D0112816

"A powerful application of recent brain science to the field of anger management. Get this book and pay attention to what it says."

—Rich Pfeiffer, MDiv, PhD, director of Growth Central

"*Healing the Angry Brain* is as thorough a work on the neurobiology of anger as you will find anywhere. In addition to a comprehensive description of the biological and psychological functions of anger, it gives lots of practical advice on regulating anger in the context of a full and healthy emotional life."

—Steven Stosny, PhD, author of *Love without Hurt, How Improve Your Marriage without Talking about It,* and *Treating Attachment Abuse*

"Psychotherapists are always asking neuroscientists, "How does understanding the brain help me to help my clients?" In *Healing the Angry Brain,* Ronald Potter-Efron provides an answer. Through a combination of clinical expertise and clear scientific information, he guides the reader to a better understanding of anger while providing a roadmap to relational and inner peace."

—Lou Cozolino, professor of psychology at Pepperdine University

HOW
UNDERSTANDING
THE WAY YOUR
BRAIN WORKS
CAN HELP YOU
CONTROL ANGER
& AGGRESSION

healing
the
angry
brain

ronald potter-efron, msw, phd

New Harbinger Publications, Inc.

Publisher's Note

This publication is designed to provide accurate and authoritative information in regard to the subject matter covered. It is sold with the understanding that the publisher is not engaged in rendering psychological, financial, legal, or other professional services. If expert assistance or counseling is needed, the services of a competent professional should be sought.

Distributed in Canada by Raincoast Books

Copyright © 2012 by Ronald Potter-Efron
             New Harbinger Publications, Inc.
             5674 Shattuck Avenue
             Oakland, CA 94609
             www.newharbinger.com

The HEALS technique is a registered trademark of Steven Stosny, PhD.

Acquired by Jess O'Brien; Edited by Jasmine Star;
Cover design by Amy Shoup; Text design by Tracy Carlson

All Rights Reserved

Library of Congress Cataloging-in-Publication Data

Potter-Efron, Ronald T.
  Healing the angry brain : how understanding the way your brain works can help you control anger and aggression / Ronald Potter-Efron.
     p. cm.
  Includes bibliographical references.
  ISBN 978-1-60882-133-4 (pbk.) -- ISBN 978-1-60882-134-1 (pdf e-book) -- ISBN 978-1-60882-135-8 (epub)
  1. Anger. 2. Control (Psychology) I. Title.
  BF575.A5.P844 2012
  152.4'7--dc23

                  2011044862

Printed in the United States of America

14   13   12

10   9   8   7   6   5   4   3   2   1   First printing

Dedicated to Lou Cozolino, my mentor, without whom I could never have written this book, and to my wife, Patricia Potter-Efron, who convinced me to try.

Contents

Acknowledgments

The first person I want to thank is my wife and frequent coauthor, Patricia Potter-Efron. It was Pat who gently but persistently encouraged me to write a book on the angry brain. Indeed, she suggested I do so about five years ago. It took three of those years for her to convince me it was something that should be done and that I could do it.

Louis Cozolino, PhD, has been my mentor and colleague throughout the process. He has reviewed every chapter and helped me avoid writing about possible brain pathways as if they were certainties. Because of Lou, I believe that everything in these pages reflects established brain science. He's been a pleasure to work with.

I wish to express my appreciation to several well-known, highly respected, and undoubtedly very busy scientists and researchers who took the time to answer my e-mails and phone calls. These include Steven Stosny, who kindly allowed me to describe his method of healing resentments in detail in chapter 4; Robert Sapolsky of Stanford University (author of *Why Zebras Don't Get Ulcers* and an expert on the linkages between fear, anger, and aggression); Allan Siegel, who has studied animal aggression for decades and has written the definitive work on the subject (*The Neurobiology of Aggression and Rage*); and Sebern Fisher, whose writings and personal communications helped me understand how neurofeedback can lessen anger. Conversations with my friend James Peterson, PhD, an expert on neurofeedback, also helped me in this regard.

I also want to thank Jess O'Brien, my editor at New Harbinger Publications, as well the entire staff at New Harbinger and founder Matthew McKay. This is my eighth book with that organization, and I continue to respect their professionalism and high standards. Thanks also to Jennifer Berger, who drew the preliminary diagrams that led to those published in this book. It has also been a pleasure working with copyeditor Jasmine Star, whose eye for both content and appearance has greatly improved the quality of the work.

As usual, my colleagues at First Things First Counseling and Consulting have been tremendously supportive: Pat Potter-Efron, Ed and Judy Ramsey, Carla Peterson, Linda Klitzke, Margo Hecker, Dave Sommers, Bruce Pamperin, Richard Fuhrer, Shawn Allen, and Pat Gaulke. Working with these wonderful people makes coming to the office a joy.

Introduction

*H*eating the Angry Brain is intended for people with angry brains. An angry brain is one that has programmed you to do some or all of these things:

- Consciously and subconsciously get angry at a moment's notice

- Become very excited and agitated when you do get angry

- Have trouble thinking or planning because your anger is so strong

- Act impulsively on your anger and frequently regret what you did afterward

- Have difficulty listening to others because you are so angry

- Hold on to your anger until you become overloaded with resentment

- Fly into dangerous rages that leave you feeling out of control of your own body

- Develop a worldview in which most or all people are perceived as enemies

Of course, an angry brain is interconnected with an angry body. Your angry brain promotes angry actions, and those behaviors in turn influence every neuron in your brain. In other words, angry brains create angry bodies, which create angry brains, in a vicious cycle that can trap you in an unnecessarily angry world. And worst of all, you might not even realize what's happening. Your angry brain has a way of convincing you that your angry thoughts, feelings, and actions are perfectly normal.

In recent decades, the brain has become a bit less mysterious. Brain scanning and imaging machines now provide much information about how the human brain's electrical and chemical systems work. However, the brain is tremendously complex. It has billions of neurons that create trillions of linkages. So it's probably safe to say that nobody really understands the human brain yet. In any case, a complete review of how the brain works is way beyond the scope of this book. Instead, I'll describe a few areas of the brain that are highly associated with anger and aggression. These areas are generally part of the limbic system, an evolutionarily older part of the brain where emotions first developed. We'll look at how the limbic system normally works to process anger effectively. And then we'll explore what can go wrong within the limbic system and other areas of the brain to potentially lead to the development of an angry brain. Most importantly, I'll suggest techniques that can help you change your brain, to end anger's dominance and to be more flexible and effective in your daily life. The goal of this book is to help you do all of the following:

- Understand what happens inside your brain when you get angry, and understand why every time you become angry your brain becomes more chronically angry.

- Learn how the brain changes and the principles of change (often called "brain plasticity") that will allow you to develop a calmer brain.

- Identify specific areas in your brain that function less than perfectly and so are at least partly responsible for creating your angry brain.

- Gain hope and motivation to change by realizing that you have the knowledge and skills to alter the way your brain works.

- Relate this information about how the brain works to the tools taught in anger management programs, such as taking time-outs and empathy training, so that you can more fully appreciate the reasons for using these skills.

- Design a personal brain retraining program that will lessen your anger and help you lead a better life.

It's only fair to warn you that making significant changes to the brain is neither fast nor simple. It will take time, energy, thought, and perseverance. You'll need to commit to a six-month program because it takes that long for the brain to redesign itself. But the payoff is well worth it. After six months of steady effort, your brain will be ready to automatically respond differently to the world. Instead of immediately presuming the worst, for example, you can train your brain to give people the benefit of the doubt. You don't have to live the rest of your life with an angry brain.

Each chapter in this book will help you take this journey toward a calmer brain. Here's an overview of the topic of each:

- **Chapter 1, Brain Basics:** This chapter presents an introduction to the basic components and processes of the brain. This will give you the background information you'll need to understand later chapters.

- **Chapter 2, The Emotional Brain:** Here I'll provide a look at how the brain handles emotions. In essence, the brain must go through six phases to handle emotions well: activation, modulation, preparation, taking action, getting feedback, and deactivation. If your brain has trouble at any of these stages, you may develop an angry brain.

- **Chapter 3, The Angry Brain:** I'll discuss specific parts of the brain that may be contributing to your anger. I'll also contrast well-handled anger and poorly handled anger. Since the brain is tremendously complex, we'll focus on the overall result of what takes place in the angry brain, rather than on the specific electrical and chemical connections that make it function.

- **Chapter 4, The Causes of an Angry Brain:** There are many factors that can cause people to become chronically angry or dangerously aggressive. Some are environmental, such as growing up with angry or abusive parents. Others are more immediate, like becoming overwhelmed with stress. Still another explanation is brain damage due to accidents or violence. This chapter will look at nine different possible causes for problematic anger.

- **Chapter 5, You Can Change Your Brain:** The brain changes according to specific rules, such as "neurons that fire together wire together." Learning these rules will help you plan how to redesign your angry brain. I'll explain how you can build, improve, and expand a neural network that will allow you to substitute the feelings and actions you want for your current angry feelings and aggressive behaviors.

- **Chapter 6, Recognizing Unconscious Anger Activation:** In general, the brain does most of its work below the level of conscious awareness. Anger is no exception. The focus of chapter 6 is on learning how the brain creates and sustains anger subconsciously. Knowing what's going on under the surface of your mind can help you develop methods for gaining better control over your anger.

- **Chapter 7, Avoiding Conscious Bad Choices:** If you often wonder why you make such lousy choices, this chapter will provide some answers. I'll discuss why angry people are prone to making bad decisions and describe several ways to improve your decision-making process.

- **Chapter 8, Developing Empathy:** Empathy—taking a caring interest in others' thoughts and feelings—is one key way to let go of anger, especially anger that has turned into resentment. Chapter 8 provides several techniques for building empathy.

Chapter 1

Brain Basics

The brain is an astonishingly complicated organ. Rather than attempting a complete review, in the following summary I'll stick to what you'll need to know to help you understand how the brain responds to potentially anger-provoking situations. In later chapters I'll describe how the brain handles anger and aggression in greater detail. You might want to reread this chapter from time to time to keep the basics in mind. As you read on, don't feel overwhelmed or distracted by the terminology; I don't expect you to become an expert on the brain. You don't even need to memorize any terms. Although I'll talk about particular areas of the brain, such as the limbic system and the prefrontal region, the main emphasis will be on how your brain does what it does when you become angry.

Basic Brain Anatomy

Your brain weighs about two to three pounds and has the consistency of soft butter. The brain can be divided into five layers. The surface layer, called the *cortex*, is sometimes referred to as the seat of the mind. The cortex is quite thin—only 1 to 4 millimeters in thickness, which means the deepest part of the cortex is less than one-sixth of an inch thick. However, it is so furrowed and ridged that its surface area amounts to two and a half square feet. Conscious thinking takes place in the cortex, including the kinds of thoughts that help people delay and inhibit angry and aggressive impulses.

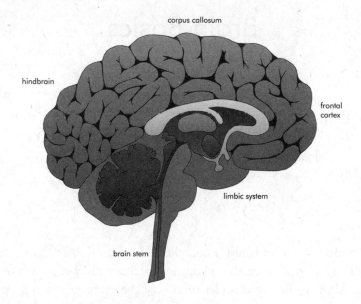

Figure 1. The structure of the brain.

The cortex is divided into two hemispheres, left and right, a situation known as *lateralization*. This allows a division of labor to occur, increasing the brain's efficiency. Each hemisphere either carries out somewhat different tasks than the other or approaches the same task in a somewhat different way. With regard to emotions, the left hemisphere is associated with positive emotions, while the right hemisphere concentrates on negative ones. Because negative emotions typically have strong survival value, it shouldn't come as a surprise that the right hemisphere develops first upon birth, with the left hemisphere becoming fully operational only in the second year of life. For people to function well, especially regarding anger and aggression management, the two hemispheres must be well integrated. The *corpus callosum*, shown in light gray in figure 1, is the main brain region that connects the two hemispheres.

Each hemisphere of the cortex is usually divided into four regions, called *lobes*, and each lobe has specialized functions. The lobes are separated by large folds in the brain that create deep valleys. The *occipital lobe*, in the back of the brain, handles visual information. The *parietal lobe*, further forward, helps us understand written language and integrate sensory information. The *temporal lobe*, located on the side of the brain, is critical for facial recognition and auditory processing. Finally, the *frontal lobe* deals with motor function, spoken language, and higher-level cognitive functions. The frontmost region of the cortex is aptly named the *prefrontal cortex* (literally, "the front of the front of the cortex"). This region is essential for anger management.

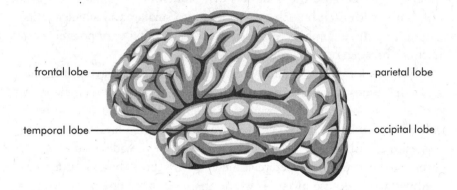

frontal lobe
parietal lobe
temporal lobe
occipital lobe

Figure 2. Lobes of the brain.

Two very important areas of the brain with regard to anger and aggression, the *thalamus* and *hypothalamus*, are located below the cortex, deeper in the brain. The thalamus organizes sensory perceptions and directs information to the cortex, while the essential job of the hypothalamus is to maintain balance, or homeostasis, within the body and brain. The hypothalamus plays a direct role in triggering acts of defensive aggression in response to perceived threats.

Another part of the brain involved with anger and aggression lies even deeper inside the skull. It is called the *periaqueductal gray* (PAG), with the "gray" reflecting that it consists of *gray matter*, the portion of the central nervous system that contains nerve cell bodies and dendrites (in contrast to white matter, which does not). As with the hypothalamus, the PAG is immediately and directly involved in displays of defensive aggression.

Neurons and Synapses

Although the brain contains many different types of cells, those of primary interest throughout this book are the *neurons*. Each neuron is composed of three segments: the *cell nucleus*; extensions of the nucleus called *dendrites*, which receive information from other neurons; and an *axon*, which delivers this information via a number of *terminals*. The eventual purpose of all of this activity is to energize and activate our major physical and mental operating systems.

The brain is estimated to contain billions of neurons. Amazingly, each of these neurons can make connections with as many as ten thousand others. That's because the dendrites can branch off multiple times, like tree limbs, with each branch subdividing into smaller and smaller units. Multiplying these numbers reveals that the total number of possible connections between neurons is in the trillions.

Neurons form long chains, with thousands of them strung together and firing almost simultaneously. Furthermore, the speed and efficiency of communication along these chains is greatly accelerated by a process called *myelinization*. Chains become myelinated when a layer of fat, called a myelin sheath, forms around the neurons to provide insulation. A myelinated pathway can operate at much faster speeds than an unmyelinated pathway. Because myelin is white, the myelinated chains of neurons are known as white matter.

Myelinization is essential; without it we can respond only slowly and tentatively to stimuli. To give you an idea just how important myelinization is, when the small cells that create myelin (oligodendrocytes) are damaged or destroyed, multiple sclerosis—an incurable condition that may cause cognitive problems and phsysical disability—is the result.

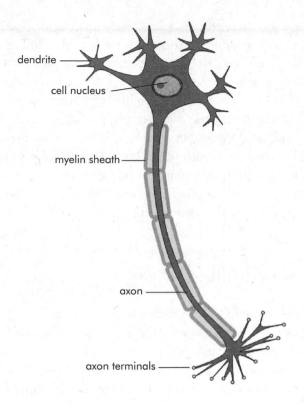

dendrite

cell nucleus

myelin sheath

axon

axon terminals

Figure 3. A myelinated neuron.

People with anger problems have usually developed deeply ingrained habits that reinforce their anger. These habits occur as the number of neurons in a network dedicated to a particular area increases over time and the connections among them become stronger. Myelinization may also contribute to habit formation by increasing the speed of message delivery. When you drive to work without even thinking about the route, you're driving along a habituated pathway in your brain. Unfortunately, the same goes for when you automatically flare up with irritation at a driver who cuts you off or at your partner trying to talk with you in the car. It is possible to break these routines, essentially by starving them through inattention and replacing them with new programs. Unfortunately, it isn't easy to do so, as you'll learn in chapter 5.

Complexity and efficiency are two standards of brain functioning. These are both maximized when neurons form interlinked systems often called *neural networks*, which can be composed of millions or even billions of neurons all linked together and firing in synchrony. Any one neuron may be part of many networks, much like a tool that can be used for many purposes. Neural networks support complexity and efficiency because neurons and *nuclei* (groups of related neurons) within these systems give ongoing information to each other in the form of feedback and "feed forward." One way to think of this is as though every neuron were a worried parent keeping track of all the kids on the playground. That neuron's motto is "Always tell me where you're going and with whom."

Neurotransmitters

The brain functions via electrochemical signals that enable it to rapidly shift from one modality to another. When a neuron receives strong enough stimulation, which usually occurs when the cell's dendrites gather excitatory information from several other cells, it fires a strong electrical signal of its own along its axon. Eventually, the resultant chain of firings directs the nervous system to take appropriate action. However, not all brain work is electrical. A critical share is chemical. That's where *neurotransmitters*, such as serotonin, dopamine, and norepinephrine, come into play. A neurotransmitter is a chemical messenger that allows one neuron to pass its message along to another. Neurotransmitters are necessary because there's a gap between the message-sending tip on the transmitting neuron's axon and the dendrites of the receiving neuron. This space, called the *synaptic gap*, cannot be crossed electrically. Instead, the cell builds and stores neurotransmitters in storage sacs known as *vesicles*. These sacs open as needed to release their stored chemicals into the space between the cells.

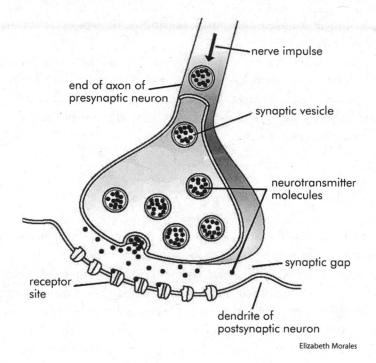

nerve impulse

end of axon of
presynaptic neuron

synaptic vesicle

neurotransmitter
molecules

synaptic gap

receptor
site

dendrite of
postsynaptic neuron

Elizabeth Morales

Figure 4. The synaptic gap.

Neurotransmitters are like swimmers crossing the English Channel. They jump off the dock at the end of the axon, swim through the ocean at a narrow spot, and land safely at a port on another neuron's dendrite so they can deliver their message. Naturally, however, it isn't that simple in the brain, given its complex structure. For one thing, the swimmer has to dock at exactly the right place with exactly the right shape (its receptor), or it cannot transmit its message. To switch analogies, think of the neurotransmitter as a key and the receptor as a lock. The key must fit exactly into the lock for the door to open and the message to be received.

Another complication is that neurotransmitters are typically released on a "just enough to do the job" principle. If too few are released or transmitted, the system weakens or shuts down completely. Perhaps the best-known example of this is some forms of biochemical depression that are thought to be caused at least in part by a scarcity of the neurotransmitter serotonin. Too much of a neurotransmitter can also cause problems. Cocaine addiction, for instance, is linked to cocaine's ability to force synaptic vesicles to release too much dopamine, thereby overexciting the brain and body.

By the way, the brain is a master recycler. It has ways to reclaim used neurotransmitters so they don't damage or clog up the system. Some neurotransmitters simply return to the originating axon and are taken up to be used again. Others are broken down within the synaptic gap so their components can be recovered.

The Role of the Limbic System

It is useful to divide the brain into three major regions based on function. The first segment of this tripartite division is the *brain stem*, which is the inner region of the brain. The brain stem is primarily responsible for maintaining core functions such as breathing, blood flow, and temperature regulation. The uppermost division is the *cerebral cortex*. This part of the brain, as previously noted, is involved in higher-level reasoning. To a greater extent than the other regions of the brain, the cortex is shaped both by genetics and by the environment. Between the brain stem and the cortex rests the *limbic system*. Actually, the limbic system contains both subcortical (below the cortex) and cortical nuclei.

The limbic system has many jobs, all of which mediate between internal, bodily reality and the external environment. You might think of the limbic system as the grand communicator. This large group of mutually responsive nuclei allows for learning, memory, and emotion regulation. The limbic system is also involved in *executive function*, a term that refers to our ability to consider possible actions, choose among them, and then act accordingly. Its role in emotion regulation is what makes the limbic system the centerpiece of any book on anger management, as the following descriptions of the regions of the limbic system make abundantly evident:

- **The amygdala,** which is actually a group of at least one dozen cell clusters, or nuclei, is best known as the site where learned fear originates. *Learned fear* occurs when something not originally dangerous is linked by association with a painful stimulus. An example would be when a buzzer goes off each time a dog is electrically shocked. Eventually the dog learns to cower at the sound of the buzzer. Less well-known is that the amygdala is equally involved in anger and aggression. Just think of the term "fight or flight" to recognize the inevitable overlap between fear and anger.

- **The hippocampus** is a relatively old part of the cortex—a fact that's recognized because the hippocampus has only three vertical layers of cells, while more recently developed regions of the brain have six vertical layers. This part of the limbic system is primarily involved in learning and memory. A well-functioning hippocampus can help you keep problems in perspective and sort out threatening from nonthreatening situations, whereas a damaged or ineffective hippocampus may do just the opposite and increase the likelihood of inappropriate overreactions.

- **The hypothalamus** regulates the sympathetic and parasympathetic branches of the autonomic (involuntary) nervous system, helping keep a balance between the stimulating function of the sympathetic nervous system and the calming function of the parasympathetic system. The hypothalamus also has a direct role in triggering defensive aggression.

- **The orbitofrontal cortex and the dorsolateral prefrontal cortex** are grouped in with the limbic system by some scientists who emphasize that humans don't either think or feel, but instead do both simultaneously, making it impossible to distinguish one from the other. Whether these two regions actually belong in the limbic system is controversial. However, they are important for anger management because they have a tremendous impact on your ability to control impulses, prioritize behavior, and understand how your actions will be received by others.

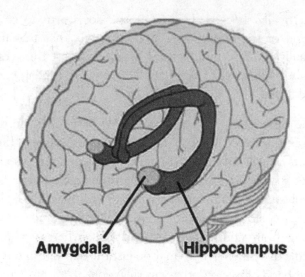

Amygdala   **Hippocampus**

Figure 5. Selected components of the limbic system.

Many scientists believe that the primary role of the newer parts of the human brain is impulse control, the reason being that it would be impossible for people to live together in families, much less larger communities, states, and nations, if we couldn't contain our aggressive and sexual impulses. The result is a mutual developmental process. As the human brain has developed over the course of evolution, so too has our ability to live together collectively; and as we have learned to live together collectively, the human brain has been spurred to grow accordingly. Our society's increasing demand for people to learn how to stay in control of their anger and aggression is a highly relevant example of how this process works.

Fortunately, the limbic system contains both lower-level nuclei with almost immediate access to pure emotion (the amygdala) and raw data (through the thalamus), as well as nuclei that can filter this data and emotion (the hippocampus, along with the orbitofrontal cortex and the dorsolateral prefrontal cortex). Utilizing these various inputs, the brain aims for just the right response to the world. Unfortunately, this balance can be difficult to achieve, and when imbalances occur, inappropriate or excessive anger can result. In the chapters that follow, we'll take a detailed look at how this happens and what you can do about it.

Summary

The brain is fascinating in its complexity. Its billions of cells are more effective and efficient than any computer. The material covered above is just a beginning look at its operations. However, this basic knowledge does allow us to go forward to explore specific ways in which anger is processed in the brain.

Chapter 2

The Emotional Brain

Emotions come in many forms: Mad, sad, glad, scared. Guilty, ashamed, embarrassed, proud. Surprised, disgusted, lonely, hurt.

This is a book about one emotion, namely anger. But before we look at anger, it's important to have a good understanding of the greater concept of emotion. What are emotions? What is so important about them? How are emotions generally processed in the brain and body? What would life be like without emotions?

What Is an Emotion?

Let's begin with a definition of emotions: Emotions are brain-generated physical and mental states that both motivate people to take action and energize their ensuing behavior. Emotions may or may not be conscious. In other words, you can have an emotion without being aware of it. Indeed, people often come under the sway of their emotions without fully realizing that they are being impacted in this way.

Emotions can linger in the background of your mind, like an orchestra playing in the distance. On the other hand, emotions can feel like a rock band blasting into your ears, insisting that you listen to them. Although emotions are usually short-term events, they can deepen into moods. A mood is essentially a "stuck" emotional state that is no longer a response to a specific event.

Emotions are generally divided into two types, depending upon the age at which they first emerge in the brain. First are the *primary emotions*: anger, fear, joy, sadness, surprise, and disgust. Primary emotions are absolutely necessary for survival, and they are hardwired in your brain. They are present and fully available at birth, as any parent of an enraged infant will attest. Each of these emotions triggers an automatic and immediate reaction or action intention.

Primary emotion	Reaction
Anger	to fight; to move against opposition; to attack
Fear	to flee; to escape
Joy	to move toward the rewarding activity; to continue
Sadness	to retrieve something that's been lost; to gather comfort from others
Surprise	to pay immediate attention; the startle response—to stop everything until you figure out what is happening
Disgust	to expel; to throw away

A bit slower to develop are the social emotions: shame, guilt, embarrassment, and pride. They probably aren't fully available until a child reaches about eighteen months of age. The purpose of social emotions is social survival: to ensure that you will be acceptable to the community in which you live. Again, each of these emotions is connected with a typical reaction.

Social emotion	Reaction
Shame	to hide; to lower yourself; to submit
Guilt	to repair damage you've done; to make amends
Embarrassment	to act appropriately; to fit in
Pride	to grow larger; to lead or dominate

While that explanation of the division between primary and social emotions sounds very clear-cut and straightforward, people seldom feel pure emotions. In real life we usually experience a blend of feelings. For instance, imagine you've just discovered that your son has become addicted to cocaine or heroin. Probably you'd feel several emotions all at once, maybe a combination of fear (*What's going to happen to him? Will he die?*), sadness (*I'm feeling like he's already gone*), anger (*I'm going to stop this nonsense right now!*), and guilt (*Am I a bad parent? What did I do wrong?*). You might feel confused with all those emotions churning around in your head. You wouldn't know what you could or should do. But hopefully eventually you'd sort through those feelings one by one and come up with an action plan appropriate to the situation.

Why Do We Have Emotions?

The reason we have emotions can be summed up in one word: survival—both physical survival and social survival. Emotions help us survive in an oftentimes threatening and dangerous world. They do so in several ways, key among them being intensification (alerting us to important signals), preparing us for action, aiding in decision making, and signaling others.

Intensification

Emotions are like loudspeakers. They amplify the strength of signals reaching us from outside or inside our bodies. They exclaim, "Pay attention! Something is going on right now that is very important!" Often this functions to alert you that you may be in danger. The stronger your emotions become, the harder they are to ignore. And that is as it should be, because bad things happen when you fail to attend to your emotional messages.

Some people don't seem to feel much emotion. The official label for this condition is alexithymia. These individuals miss a lot of critical messages. They often sense that they're losing out on life because they stay cool even when they should be warming up. For instance, they might only feel slightly pleased when their child is born instead of feeling overwhelming joy. It's like a painter using only shades of gray. Their emotional life is flat and dull.

On the other hand, nobody can endure endless intensification. Emotions are hard on the body and soul. Emotions are normally short-term messengers, more like sprinters than marathon runners. That's good, because when the danger subsides, the emotions that alerted you to it should diminish accordingly. If they don't, you may have a problem. (I'll discuss difficulties with letting go of emotions later in this chapter and later in the book.)

Intensification is one job that anger does well. It's almost as if anger were a messenger telling you to pay attention, right now, because something is going wrong in your life. It's usually important and healthy to listen to that inner message.

Preparation for Action

Remember that each emotion typically evokes an automatic reaction. These hardwired action programs put the "motion" in emotion. (In fact, the Latin root of the word "emotion" means "to move.") If we didn't have the ability to control our impulses, then as soon as we felt an emotion we'd immediately spring into action. We'd run at the first glimmer of fear, fight at the drop of a hat, actually cry over spilled milk, and so on. And indeed, this is how people who have impulse control problems react: Their emotions trigger actions too quickly. When anger is their issue, they say they have a short fuse or a quick trigger. What's happening, as I'll discuss in detail later, is that their emotional reaction has short-circuited the frontal region of the brain. No frontal region involvement means no impulse control, which means hair-trigger emotions, and that spells trouble.

For now, let's look at how emotions help us prepare for action from a positive perspective. Could you imagine walking onstage to receive your high school or college diploma without feeling any emotion? If you weren't feeling deservedly proud, you probably would have found an excuse to avoid going through all the hassle of the graduation ceremony. Or what if you were walking across the street and suddenly saw a tractor-trailer hurtling toward you? It would certainly be critical to feel that jolt of adrenaline accompanying your awareness that you were in immediate danger. This is no time to linger or to ponder your predicament. When it's time for action, your emotions help you do what you need to do to survive.

With anger, it's extremely important to be cautious with how it prepares you for action. When people tell me about their anger, I typically say, "Okay, you're angry. It's good that you're telling me this. But what are you planning to do now that you're angry? Is there something constructive you can do to help fix the problem so you can let go of your anger?"

Decision Making

Emotions are vital in decision-making situations. "Should I marry her?" "Should I leave him and the kids?" "Should I move to California?" "Should I quit drinking?" "Should I go to an anger management class?" When faced with such important questions, how can you decide what to do?

One tactic is to make a list of all the pros and cons for a given course of action. Let's take a look at how this pans out with the marriage question.

Pros

- She's attractive.

- She's smart.

- She has a keen sense of humor.

- She wants children like I do.

- She takes a real interest in me.

Cons

- She's twelve years older than me.

- She has a temper.

- She wants to move to California.

- She already has a child who doesn't want me around.

- She doesn't like to talk about her feelings.

Okay, what's the result? It looks sort of like a toss-up. The reality is, you can't make up your mind on facts alone. No matter how compelling the facts, you can't decide much of anything until you allow emotions to enter the equation. You have to ask yourself these kinds of questions: "Which of the facts that I wrote down really matter to me?" "What feelings do I have when I read each fact?" "Of all the items I listed, which one do I feel most strongly about?" If the most critical item turns out to be that this woman has a mean temper that scares you and turns you off, then you probably shouldn't marry her (at least not until the two of you have had a heart-to-heart talk about her anger). But if the fact that she takes a real interest in you is pivotal, if that makes you feel really special and joyful, then hurry up and buy that ring!

Anger certainly helps people make important decisions. It's not unusual for people to say that they put up with physical or emotional abuse for years until they finally became angry enough to leave.

Signaling Others

The last major job for emotions is interpersonal. Humans are exceptional creatures because we show a wide range of emotions with our faces and bodies. Others know when you are happy, mad, scared, sad, ashamed, or proud. They know because you deliver a message about your emotions through your facial expression and body language. And because others can read your emotions, they can respond accurately to your needs and desires.

Yet something even more dramatic occurs when you show an emotion to someone else. Humans, along with other primates, are capable of *empathy*, which means we are able to imagine ourselves in another person's shoes. Not only can we imagine someone else's situation, we can actually feel at least a part of what that person is experiencing. So if you see me crying, you may feel like crying yourself. My sadness triggers a similar emotional reaction in you. Of course we are each unique, so nobody can feel exactly what another feels. But my emotion can trigger something close enough in you that you can then respond more accurately to my message.

Intensity, preparation, and decision making get communicated to others through your emotions and help others understand what you are trying to communicate. If my eyebrows dip, my mouth turns down at the edges, and my eyes seem to narrow into a glare, you can not only tell that I'm angry, but also have a good idea how angry I am (intensity), what I might do (preparation), and how close I am to action (decision making). The bottom line is that emotions are both a personal and a social event.

Here too anger is a valuable resource. If you let others know that you're angry with them, they can alter their behavior. But if others don't receive the signal that you're angry, they may not know they've offended you.

The Six Stages of Emotional Processing

The human brain is an incredibly complex organ. As mentioned in chapter 1, it's estimated that there are billions of neurons within the brain, with trillions of connections between them. Needless to say, no one can truly comprehend this level of intricacy, so any discussion of brain processes will by necessity be a simplification—including what I've written about the emotional or angry brain. For instance, it won't be possible to indicate every single feedback mechanism (where part B of the brain, which has just been stimulated by part A, tells part A that it has had just the right amount of stimulation, thank you very much; or not quite enough, so it requests a bit more; or maybe a little too much, so it requests that part A quit stimulating it for a while). The brain never functions without these feedback mechanisms, but it would take hundreds of pages to even begin to describe them. So instead, I'll try to concentrate on the brain's best-researched, easiest-to-understand, and most relevant mechanisms and interactions.

Let's consider this approach with the general theme of the emotional brain. I'm about to present a six-stage model of what the brain needs to do in order to fully process an emotional event. I'll describe these stages as if they happen in a nice, linear manner. In terms of internal communication, that means I need to describe a total of five connections, one between each stage: A talks to B, then B talks to C, and so on. But that's not how the brain works. The reality is more like A talks to B, C, D, E, and F; B talks to A, C, D, E, and F; and so on. This means I'd have to describe a total of thirty connections. Furthermore, after A talks to B, then B might want to pass the message along to C, D, E, or F (or, for that matter, all of them). Now the connections reach into the hundreds and thousands. That's why explanations of brain functions must be simplified to some extent: to make the information manageable.

Although simplification is a necessity, the goal is to simplify without becoming simplistic. Ultimately, any description must reflect the essential truths of this complex system, or it will be useless. And that is what I'll try to do in terms of the six-stage model of emotional processing. In later chapters I'll describe the brain mechanics of this process in relation to anger. For now, I'll simply acquaint you with the model (illustrated in figure 6).

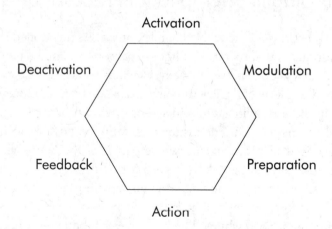

Figure 6. The six stages of an emotional episode.

Stage 1: Activation

Activation occurs whenever something happens that initiates an emotional event. The immediate activator might be an external event, such as someone shouting at you, your pet running into the street, a driver giving you the finger, someone telling you that you just did something poorly, or hitting the jackpot at a casino. It might also be something internal, such as thinking about the death of a friend, your hopes for the future, or a mistake you made on a craft project. Internal activators can be about something from your past or future, not just the present.

One important reminder: The emotion or its activator may be beneath your conscious awareness. You don't have to know you're having an emotional reaction in order to have one. Indeed, people often experience subtle emotional events that never reach their full awareness. Sometimes you may find yourself reacting to emotions before you're aware that you're feeling anything at all; for instance, your eyes might begin tearing up seconds before you consciously start thinking about your lost dog.

It's also possible for unconscious emotions to be in conflict with your desired conscious state. One vivid example I remember involved a man named Floyd, whom I once counseled. He swore he wasn't at all angry about an insult he'd recently received, yet his hands were making fists. When I pointed out what his hands were doing, Floyd's reaction was to put his hands behind his back and continue to assert that he felt calm.

Even when we believe we are fully conscious of our emotions, they are almost certainly still operating at partially unconscious levels. Our past experiences, personality characteristics, and temperament all play a part in what types of emotional material remain unconscious or become partly or fully conscious.

In the field of psychotherapy, there is a tradition of bringing the unconsciousness into consciousness that can be traced all the way back to its founder, Sigmund Freud. One of my most essential tasks as an anger management counselor is to help people become aware of the early signs of hidden, subconscious emotions. Bringing greater awareness to these signs and emotions gives people time to intervene and inhibit their anger.

Certain events activate almost everybody's emotions. These stimuli inevitably are related to our primary emotions. Who wouldn't have a strong reaction to the sight of a mother bear charging headfirst at you in defense of her cubs? But most potential emotional activators are far from universal. While some people feel sad that loved ones have passed away, others profess a calm faith that the separation is only temporary and that they will soon meet again in heaven. What is there to be sad about, they ask, when they know their loved ones are in a better place?

Which events (internal as well as external) activate your emotions depends upon many factors. For example, your genetic background has a bearing on how sensitive you are to emotional triggers. Personal history also plays a role, such as in a rape victim's fear of dark places. Social and cultural expectations are involved, as well; for example, traditional Latin cultures expect and allow more and stronger emotional displays than traditional Scandinavian cultures. In addition, the specific emotions triggered by an event vary from person to person. While some people might mostly feel angry upon discovering that their partner betrayed them, others might primarily experience sadness. The main point, however, is that one or more emotions have become activated in the first stage of an emotional episode.

Stage 2: Modulation

Once your emotional system has been activated, the next important issue is how strongly you should respond. Remember that intensification is one of the major functions of emotion. Your emotions allow you to prioritize incoming information regarding exactly how critical a situation is. The range of responses can vary from "That's sort of interesting" to "Oh my god, this is huge!"

Cognitive therapists have understood this concept for years. That's why they ask clients to rate their thoughts on a scale of 0 to 10. For instance, a 2 translates to "This is annoying but not serious," while 6 means "I'd better pay serious attention to this problem," and 10 is reserved for immediate life-threatening circumstances. A similar scale can be applied to emotions. In this case, a 2 indicates "I'm feeling something, but it's not very strong," 6 means "I'm definitely feeling the heat," and 10 indicates "This is so intense I can barely stand it."

An interesting situation arises when your thought score doesn't match your emotional score. Imagine, for instance, discovering that your beautiful beagle just dug a big hole in your neighbors' yard. You might rate that as a 7 on the cognitive scale because you know your neighbors are going to get fairly upset about the damage. Emotionally, though, you only feel a 3. After all, that's what dogs do, isn't it? They dig. Besides, you don't like your neighbors, so it's hard to feel much sympathy toward them and their lawn. Or it could go the other way. Cognitively you give this event a 2 because it's not a very big hole and it's way on the edge of your neighbor's property, but emotionally you give it a 9 because you're deathly afraid of anyone's anger.

Whenever there's a significant gulf between your cognitive and emotional reactions to an event, it's likely that you'll feel confused and uncertain. You won't know whether to act according to the stronger reaction, the weaker one, or somewhere in between. However, based on my experience as a therapist, when there's a conflict between the intensity of thoughts and emotions, I'd bet on people acting in a way that reflects their emotional score every time. Emotions are very powerful predictors of action—much more so than thoughts.

Accurate modulation is critical for good anger management. Simply put, it's a recipe for disaster when you inaccurately exaggerate the threats around you and therefore feel needlessly endangered.

Stage 3: Preparation

Preparation is the third stage of the natural sequence of an emotional episode as it takes place in the brain and body. The purpose of this stage is to get ready for action.

Much of this preparation is automatic and beneath awareness or conscious choice. At this point your brain has already ordered your endocrine, or hormonal, system and central nervous system to get moving, particularly if your brain has sensed any sort of danger. For example, your adrenal glands will have begun producing cortisol, a hormone that facilitates a rapid response to threat.

Let's focus upon what happens with anger during the preparation phase. Since anger is frequently a response to a perceived threat, your body tends to react powerfully whenever you become angry. Your heart rate accelerates, and your blood pressure may increase dramatically. The purpose of these changes is to supply more blood to your arms and legs so you'll be ready to fight or flee. Sometimes your blood might flow so strongly that it causes the tiny blood vessels in your eyes to expand. That's when people report that they literally see red. Perhaps it's evident to you that these physiological reactions significantly increase your vulnerability to a heart attack or stroke. This is one reason many cardiologists encourage their patients to enroll in anger management counseling. In addition, the airways in your lungs open more to allow increased oxygen intake and your digestive system comes to a screeching halt.

Not all preparation takes place subconsciously, though. Normally you'll also have a little time to think. Unfortunately, thinking at this stage is seldom a purely objective process. Your thoughts are colored by your physical and emotional state. Imagine, for example, that you're in a meeting at work and one of your coworkers verbally attacks you. Maybe he says that you don't know what you're doing and are totally messing up the project you've been working on together. Do you believe your reaction will be totally fair, rational, controlled, and calm? It might be—if you're really good at stuffing your anger and maintaining a cool appearance. But even then you'll be plenty angry; you just won't show it. However, I think it's likely that your response will be more volatile. You're likely to become defensive and to counterattack angrily.

Nevertheless, the preparation stage offers you a good opportunity to figure out how to use your anger well, especially if you take the time to calm down a bit before acting. That time will allow the frontal lobes of your brain to respond to whatever has triggered your anger. Later we'll discuss the specific regions in the frontal lobes that are most helpful for inhibiting immediate strong reactions to anger triggers.

Stage 4: Action

I used to think of emotions primarily as messengers. They would tell us that it was important to notice something and then go away. Then the brain's action centers would take over the job of keeping us safe. But I wasn't taking the "motion" part of emotion into consideration. Emotions don't merely prepare us for action; they are part of the action itself.

Here's an example: Let's say you buy an elliptical trainer or some other expensive exercise equipment. You set it up in your spare room. You read the manual. You see that you need to work out at least three times a week in order to see results. You do that faithfully—for about four weeks. After that the machine gathers dust for a couple of years until you get rid of it during a garage sale. Later you say the equipment was a good idea, but you simply couldn't get motivated enough to use it regularly.

What happened? You had a great idea, but, unfortunately, you apparently didn't consult your emotions before you purchased that expensive equipment. If you had, they would have told you that they weren't interested in exercising. In particular, your positive emotional center, usually located on the left side of the brain (the dominant side for most right-handed people), didn't respond. You didn't feel enough positive satisfaction to counter the physical exhaustion you were voluntarily experiencing. So, instead of a "Yes, this feels good" reaction, you felt a "Yuck, this is painful" reaction. It's natural to quit doing something that feels intrinsically unsatisfying.

You'll see just how important emotions are in creating long-term change, including letting go of excessive anger and aggression, when we take a look at the brain's remarkable ability to change in chapter 5.

So emotions inform our actions. The danger is that you'll overreact if you have an overly strong emotional response to a situation. If so, you may say or do things you will later deeply regret.

Stage 5: Feedback

Emotions don't stop abruptly once you've taken action. They still have an important job to do: they must give you feedback so you'll know whether your action was useful and appropriate.

To see how this works, consider Jolene and Frank, who have been struggling with their relationship for about a year. They've both worked hard to improve their life together, but nothing seems to work. Finally, Jolene tells Frank she just can't do it anymore, that she feels physically and emotionally exhausted and wants a separation. Frank agrees and he moves out immediately. It's over, isn't it? If your answer is "No, it's not over. Life is never that simple," you're probably correct.

Jolene's emotional response is one of great relief. She can relax. Her sadness subsides and she feels less irritable. She soon begins to have moments of happiness again, a feeling that had gone missing for months. Her emotional feedback translates into "Yes, you did the right thing. Stick with the plan." Frank, however, receives entirely different emotional feedback. His sadness deepens toward depression. It's almost as if his feelings are telling him that he can't go on—he can't proceed with life. Frank's emotional feedback translates into "No, you've made a big mistake. You've got to try to save your relationship with Jolene."

As previously mentioned, the brain is a master of feedback. Every action we take, every thought we think, every emotion we feel is reviewed. This feedback process allows us to recognize and repair our actions when we've committed a serious error. More frequently, though, feedback helps us refine our actions, thoughts, and feelings. Gradually we get better at what we do, how we think, and what we feel—all thanks to the brain's ongoing ability to inspect its creations.

We can also receive feedback from others. Family members, friends, colleagues, neighbors, and others we interact with all react to our actions, helping us learn whether the choices we've made are appropriate and effective. Their feedback can take the form of words, facial expressions, gestures, or actions.

Stage 6: Deactivation

Emotions are normally time-limited processes. This is particularly true for anger, which tends to occur in abrupt and discrete episodes. Sadness, in contrast, usually develops more like a wave on the ocean and typically lasts longer than anger. Even so, as you know if you've experienced grief, the sadness waxes and wanes, and sometimes there are periods when you don't feel sad at all. In general, emotions are deactivated when the stimulus that triggered the emotion has been handled or has gone away.

Emotional deactivation is necessary for energy efficiency. The brain is an energy hog, using far more than its share of glucose, the main source of energy in the body. Emotion takes energy, and energy demands calories. Naturally, then, your brain will shut down emotions when there is no need for them. That's why people exist in a state of emotional neutrality most of the time. If you want to see proof of this, just walk through the departure level of an airport. Nobody shows much emotion at that level. Go down a floor, however, where returning passengers are greeted by their family and friends, and you'll see a far more emotional scene.

When people ask how we're doing when we're in neutral, we may reply, "Fine." What "fine" means in this situation is "I'm okay. Nothing bad is happening. There's no reason for alarm." Admittedly, it's a bit of an exaggeration to say that we're often emotionally neutral. It would be more accurate to say that we maintain some emotional alertness at all times, but it's usually in the form of a subtle background state—a general sense of comfort or discomfort, pleasure or displeasure, or contentment or discontent.

Emotional deactivation allows the brain to rest and prepare for the next cycle of emotions. The process is completed so it can be reactivated again when needed.

Well-Handled Emotions

I recently attended a jewelry-making session in which my teacher, Don Norris, helped me design and create a silver-framed turquoise pendant. In essence we flowed through the six stages described above. For instance, when it came time to solder one piece of silver to another, I activated the episode by lighting my torch, modulated the flame by changing its strength, prepared the work carefully by placing the pieces where they needed to be, took action by bringing the torch to the silver, got feedback from my mentor ("Steady, Ron, hold the torch steady!"), and then deactivated by extinguishing the flame. Success!

Making jewelry is a snap compared to dealing with feelings. But you will have just as much success with emotions when you carefully proceed through the six stages described above. In chapter 3, I'll describe well-handled anger in detail. For now, here's an outline of well-handled emotion using fear as an example:

Stage 1: Well-handled activation. Your activation system goes on for a good reason. For instance, you're outside your house on a stormy day and suddenly you hear a loud sound like a train quickly approaching. Your startle reaction keeps you from moving for a few seconds while you search for the source of the noise. Meanwhile, your body is already readying itself for action.

Stage 2: Well-handled modulation. Your startle reaction gives way to fear. As the noise rapidly gets louder, you spot a tornado. It's coming at you. You feel a surge of terror. On a scale from 0 to 10, you'd give it a score of 10. This is a life-threatening situation.

Stage 3: Well-handled preparation. Your brain and body are now in full agreement: *Run!*

Stage 4: Well-handled action. You dash into your home and dive into the basement.

Stage 5: Well-handled feedback. The tornado passes within yards of where you'd been standing outside. You might have been killed if you had stayed there. You realize you did the right thing.

Stage 6: Well-handled deactivation. It might take a few hours, but eventually your heart quits racing. Your fear subsides. Life gets back to normal.

Poorly Handled Emotions

There would be no need for this book if every emotional situation were the equivalent of a tornado. But real life is typically far more complex and subtle. Emotional situations can be ambiguous and confusing. Furthermore, no one is blessed with a perfect brain, and imperfect brains produce imperfect responses to difficult situations. A natural consequence of this situation is that we often commit emotional errors. These mistakes can occur at any of the six stages of emotional processing. I'll briefly describe some common types of mistakes at each stage for emotions in general below. We'll get into the details in chapter 3.

Stage 1: Poorly Handled Activation

Two kinds of mistakes are possible at the activation stage. First, the system can fail to activate when it should. Imagine what would happen if you were so engrossed in your gardening project, so enamored of your tomatoes, that you failed to hear the tornado approaching.

The second activation mistake happens when the system becomes too good at what it does and you become hypersensitive. This can happen with one emotion, such as fear; many negative emotions; or even all emotions. You might start hearing so many imaginary tornado sounds that you stay inside all summer.

People are more likely to seek help for overactivation problems than underactivation problems: the overactivation of fear that leads to panic attacks, the overactivation of sadness that produces depressive symptoms, and perhaps the overactivation of joy that triggers manic episodes. And given that you're reading this book, you will doubtless agree that overactivation of anger can get people into a lot of trouble.

One source of overactivation is the amygdala, which has a power that belies its small size. An overactive or damaged amygdala is a well-known cause of excessive fearfulness. Less understood is that it is also a source of hypersensitivity to anger.

Stage 2: Poorly Handled Modulation

Ideally, we should all react to each emotional situation with exactly the right amount of intensity. But, like the oatmeal Goldilocks tastes at the Three Bears' house, a reaction may be a little too cold, a little too hot, or just right.

When you underreact, you fail to muster a sufficiently robust emotional response to a trigger. If underreacting becomes a habitual pattern, then you'll go through life as if your mantra were "It's no big deal." Like a numbed-out gambler at a casino who stone-facedly keeps pushing the button of a gaming machine regardless of whether he's winning or losing, nothing will get you excited.

When you respond with too much heat, you set yourself up to overreact. Can you think which children's story describes people who overreact to emotional triggers? Chicken Little, of course, the hysterical bird whose shouts that "the sky is falling" would earn her a prescription for strong antianxiety medications these days. Some people consistently overreact to specific emotional triggers, such as fear or shame, whereas others are overly responsive to emotional triggers in general.

The hippocampus, like the amygdala, is also a relatively small area in the brain. Despite its small size, a well-functioning hippocampus helps you accurately modulate your emotional state. And based on animal studies, it appears that the hippocampus (along with the septal region) is a critical player in turning off aggression (Siegel 2005). But as you'll learn in chapter 4, the hippocampus is susceptible to damage as a result of stressful events. That damage can lead to errors in modulation.

Stage 3: Poorly Handled Preparation

Let's start thinking cumulatively. If you're oversensitive to emotional triggers at stage 1 and then get too heated up at stage 2, you can probably imagine what will happen as you continue through the cycle. You'll be like a driver trying to figure out the best route across unfamiliar territory while holding an outdated map upside down and driving one hundred miles per hour. There's no way you'll be able to rationally sort through your options to plan out the best possible itinerary.

As if that weren't bad enough, some people have particular brain difficulties at stage 3 that only make things worse. These difficulties are called *executive control problems*. They reflect the inability of the frontal lobes to exert enough influence over the more primitive emotional centers to keep them under control. This is especially an issue with anger problems, if only because angry people tend to seek quick and dirty solutions to problems. In any case, it's probably safe to say that clear thinking is never easy in the midst of a strong emotional experience.

Remember, though, that emotion plays a crucial role in making important decisions. So here's another emotional processing problem: If you don't feel strongly about any of the alternatives, you'll have trouble at the preparation stage. You won't be able to decide on a plan—even if doing so is essential.

Stage 4: Poorly Handled Action

As mentioned in chapter 2, every emotion includes a template for an automatic reaction. So a feeling isn't just a feeling; it's also a movement or at least a potential movement: With fear you may want to run. Shame makes you want to hide. Anger might compel you to attack. Joy makes you want to approach. Ideally, if things go well through the first three stages of an emotional episode, in stage 4 you're primed to take appropriate action, directed at the right person with exactly the correct level of intensity. But even under the best of circumstances, people can and do make predictable mistakes at the action stage. Sometimes we fire blanks, and at other times the gun explodes in our face. Occasionally we don't fire at all; for instance, when we become paralyzed with fear.

I often think the healthy brain's motto must be "Moderation in all things." That is certainly true for the action stage of emotional processing. You can pay a huge price if you either undershoot or overshoot, so your brain wants you to make exactly the right response. Neurotransmitters, the brain's chemical messengers discussed in chapter 1, play a huge role here. Some of them help you initiate actions or increase your activity level, while others reduce your activity level or even stop you from taking action. When everything goes well, neurotransmitters help you achieve a good balance between activity and inactivity. However, an imbalance among neurotransmitters can produce problems at the action stage.

People often seek counseling or therapy because they can't take action even when they know they should. One of the most serious such circumstances occurs when battered spouses cannot quite pull it together to get out of harm's way. They usually feel strongly about the situation yet cannot act. This impasse may be the result of strong but conflicting emotions—an unresolved battle between love and fear. In such cases, therapy involves helping these people sort through their options by discussing all of their emotions without judgment.

Impulsivity is another problem that occurs at the action stage. Indeed, impulsive anger and aggression are serious problems. Impulsive people seem to jump from activation to action, bypassing the modulation and preparation stages. As you'll soon see, one neurotransmitter is particularly important for effective impulse control: serotonin.

Stage 5: Poorly Handled Feedback

Earlier, I shared the story of my recent adventure in creating turquoise jewelry, in which I made an attractive pendant. Do you believe I could do that all on my own the first time I tried? No way. I have few skills and less experience when it comes to any sort of craftsmanship. But what I did have was an excellent teacher. "Try it this way," he'd suggest. "Let me show you how" was Don's rescue line for when I was really screwing up. He regularly gave me, my wife, Pat, and the other participants timely and useful information. Still, any bit of feedback from others, no matter how kindly offered, must run the gamut of the recipient's emotional response habits. What if I had interpreted Don's "Try it this way" as "He's saying that I don't know anything" or his "Let me show you how" as if he were calling me a moron? If I had, Don's perfectly innocent statements would have triggered a shame response in me that could have led to various inappropriate actions: I might have gone into hiding by saying nothing but secretly giving up; I could have started calling myself names like "stupid" and "dummy"; or I might have become irate and defensively attacked him. My shame-based, distorted perception of his intent could have doomed me to make an unfortunate and relationship-damaging mistake.

Luckily, the brain possesses one tremendous skill that lessens the likelihood of making this kind of feedback miscalculation. I mentioned this skill earlier in this chapter. It's empathy. Your empathic response puts you in the shoes of someone else. Then you're less likely to project your own emotions onto others. You'll see them as they really are. You'll more fully understand the meaning of their words and deeds. You'll be able to relate more accurately to their emotions.

One of the more exciting areas of recent brain research is *mirror neurons*. These brain cells react to others' intentional actions in precisely the manner as when you yourself perform those same actions. Mirror neurons may underlie the phenomenon of empathy, though much research will be required to determine whether this is actually the case.

Empathy is a higher-level mental function. It involves particular regions of the brain's prefrontal cortex. While the potential to feel empathy may exist from birth, it is a skill that must be developed with practice. That effort pays off many times over if you have an anger problem, because the more empathy you develop toward someone, the harder it becomes to feel anger, resentment, or hatred toward that person. (Chapter 8 will discuss empathy in detail.)

Stage 6: Poorly Handled Deactivation

As mentioned before, emotions are usually time limited. They appear, serve their purpose, and fade away. "Deactivation" is the term I use for the last stage in emotional processing, during which emotions recede and are replaced with emotional neutrality. Even here, an emotional episode can go awry.

It's possible to deactivate too quickly. Here's an example: Sal has a serious drinking problem. His wife, Peggy, and various family members hold an intervention. It's an emotional scene, of course, and Peggy's high levels of fear, sadness, and anger help her confront Sal. Deeply touched, Sal agrees to go into inpatient treatment. But by the next day Peggy's intensity level has fallen dramatically. Gone are the fear, sadness, and anger. Now she starts to think about the hassle of getting to work and caring for their kids with Sal gone for a few weeks. So Peggy tells him that he doesn't have to go into treatment after all—that he just needs to promise to try to drink less. Needless to say, Sal happily agrees. You can guess the result.

Deactivating too slowly, so that emotions hang on long after they are no longer needed, is also a problem. An example would be feeling scared hours after you jumped out of the way of an oncoming bus, or not letting go of a sense of loneliness even while you're surrounded by friends. In the world of anger, you may store resentments as if they were precious jewels, frequently taking them out to caress them. If you don't let go of your emotions, you can't finish the emotional cycle. You're stuck.

Summary

The six stages of an emotional cycle apply to all emotions. At each stage, your brain can help you feel and do things just right, or it can cause you to react excessively or insufficiently. Now that you have a good understanding of how a basic emotional episode evolves, the next chapter will discuss how this cycle applies specifically to anger.

Chapter 3

The Angry Brain

In the previous chapter, I described some of the ways emotions can be handled well or mishandled in each of six stages of an emotional episode. In this chapter I'll zero in on anger and discuss how it can be processed well or poorly. But first, let's take a look at the mechanics of how the brain handles anger and aggression.

Cats, Rats, and Humans

Until the late 1990s, it was very difficult to study the human brain. Fortunately, scientists now have many new tools that allow for direct investigation of the brain. They can study the brain's electrical conveyance patterns with electroencephalograms and similar methods. They can study blood flow through the brain with single-photon emission computed tomography (SPECT) imagery. Computed tomography (CT) scans can pick up brain tumors. Positron-emission tomography (PET) scans map glucose usage in the brain, indirectly demonstrating which areas of the brain are active under certain conditions (for example, during periods of anger and aggression). Researchers can also use a multitude of medications and chemical preparations to alter behavior. More recent developments are even more spectacular, as scientists can now pinpoint and measure brain activity at microscopic levels, up to and including single neurons. Most importantly, much of this research can be done noninvasively.

Scientists from previous eras didn't have the luxury of these remarkable modern methods of investigation. Consequently, they had to rely upon live animals and human cadavers to study the brain. Occasionally they could also glean information from living humans who had survived certain types of head injuries. By far the most famous case is that of Phineas Gage, a steadfast and reliable railroad worker who survived an accident in which an explosion sent a tamping rod right through his frontal lobe. Gage was blinded in one eye, but that was far from the worst of what happened. According to some accounts (which may have exaggerated the effects of this accident upon Gage's personality), he also became emotionally and behaviorally unstable. He was never able to work regularly again, and he eventually became a drifter. People who knew him bemoaned his personality changes, while doctors and scientists were able to see how damage to his frontal cortex not only negatively affected his reasoning ability but also damaged his ability to control his emotions.

Still, animal studies have been and remain the cornerstone for research about anger and aggression. Although many creatures have been scrutinized, the bulk of research has used cats and rats as subjects. Rats are often chosen for studies because they are similar to humans in many ways, and because of their brief life span, they can be studied over many generations. As for cats, any feline owner knows that they display aggressive behaviors regularly and highly visibly.

One obvious difficulty with animal studies is that scientists can't ask cats or rats how they feel. They can, however, watch what animals do when they are intentionally provoked. Scientists can ascertain when and how an animal reacts with aggression. They can also discern when and how animals manage to inhibit aggression. They can manipulate the animal brain with medications to discover which chemicals increase or decrease the ability to inhibit aggression, and this information certainly has a bearing on impulse control issues.

At this point, you may be wondering whether animal studies can tell us much about human behavior. I believe that animal studies on anger and aggression are limited but useful. They say something, but not everything, about how people behave. Although the human brain is very complex and human behavior is equally intricate, animal studies do point out useful directions for study in humans.

Given the state of the science, I recommend that you keep in mind that the information I present about the brain isn't gospel truth. Scientists still don't know enough about how the human brain processes anger and aggression to make many definitive statements. And as scientific tools improve, some of today's claims will be displaced by new and better information. This is particularly true in regard to the emotion of anger as opposed to the behavior of aggression. Remember, though, that emotions always include a motivation to act. It's not really possible to separate the feeling of anger from the action of aggression. Although we may choose to emphasize one or the other, feelings and actions are ultimately parts of the same package.

Before continuing, I want to offer a neutral interpretation of aggression. Many people think of aggression as a negative trait, a bad thing that should be eliminated in human interaction. Others think of aggression as a good thing, something to be encouraged so you can defend yourself from attack. I suggest that aggression simply is a fact of life, neither intrinsically good nor intrinsically bad. It just is. For humans, aggression becomes a positive tool when used appropriately (according to the rules of the society in which you reside). It becomes negative when you break societal rules, norms, and expectations by displaying aggression in the wrong situation or for the wrong reasons.

Predatory vs. Defensive Aggression

One of the most important findings that has emerged from animal studies is that there is a distinction between predatory and defensive aggression. Most importantly, these two types of aggression follow different pathways in the brain. This distinction is more evident in higher primates than in less-developed animals, so it probably applies to humans as well.

Predatory aggression takes place when an animal goes on the hunt. Apparently, this type of aggression doesn't involve what we would normally call emotion. It is more a case of business as usual. Animals hunt to live. They aren't angry at their prey. In fact hunting is hardly a time for feelings. When hunting, animals need physical excitement because tracking down and killing prey requires a lot of energy. But excitement is different from emotion. Despite that excitement, the hunter needs to be "cold" rather than "hot" in its approach to dinner. Just think of a cat watching, waiting, ready to pounce. Its twitching tail is the cat's only outward indication of the potential energy it's ready to unleash.

Here's an amazing research discovery: Many animals (and probably humans) cannot simultaneously fire up both predatory and defensive aggression (Siegel 2005). The brain insists that only one of these programs be activated at a time. It's similar to how you can't drive a car while simultaneously pressing the accelerator and the brake pedal. Likewise, imagine the problems a lioness would run into trying to attack a zebra through predatory aggression while also protecting herself from danger through defensive aggression. That lioness would find herself paralyzed into inaction and incapable of either hunting or defending herself.

Here's how this either-or switch works. In animal and human brains the widespread neurotransmitter GABA (shorthand for gamma-aminobutyric acid) serves as a general action inhibitor. Its counterpart is glutamate, an activating neurotransmitter. Aggression is just one of many kinds of behavior for which GABA and glutamate perform their tasks of inhibition and activation. The key point here, though, is that GABA automatically turns off whichever aggression mechanism—predatory or defensive—is inappropriate in a particular situation. Isn't this a beautiful demonstration of how the brain manipulates itself to focus upon the specific task that needs attention at any given moment?

Before we move on to the central topic here—defensive aggression—let's briefly look at whether humans ever exhibit the characteristics of predatory aggression. I can think of two contexts in which this might occur. The first is easy for me to imagine because I live in rural Wisconsin, home of dairy farms, forested hilltops, and tens of thousands of deer. Every fall, droves of people engage in deer hunting. I'm not a hunter myself, but my son-in-law Mark is avid about it, as are many of my friends. I never used to believe these people when they said they hunted without anger; I thought it was impossible to kill an animal without anger. But now that I've learned about the distinction between predatory and defensive anger, I do believe what they say.

The other possible context for human predatory aggression is more controversial. Do sociopaths, who seemingly rob, kidnap, rape, and kill other human beings without remorse, qualify? Do they actually look at others simply as prey? We certainly call people like these predators for a reason. However, I recommend caution here until definitive studies are completed. It is possible that at least some apparently pitiless individuals do feel remorse (which is primarily the feeling of guilt), at least at an unconscious level. Besides, guilt is a social emotion, not a primary emotion. Perhaps people who don't feel remorse still feel anger, fear, and other primary emotions when engaged in predatory behavior. Maybe that's why they often fail so glaringly—because their primary emotions cause them to plan poorly or act ineffectively.

I've worked with many people whom I would label "recovering sociopaths." These individuals have grown out of their sociopathic period (always with the help of age, and frequently with the help of prison time). Some of them report that they felt nothing for their victims. Others say they felt badly at the time but didn't dare say so. Most say they now feel remorse over what they did in the past. Perhaps some of those who express remorse are trying to scam me or the world. But many of these individuals not only go straight but also turn to careers in which they can assist others in ending their sociopathic behaviors. In my view, this means that people who appear remorseless shouldn't be treated as hopeless creatures to be locked away forever. And based on my experiences, I urge caution in labeling anyone as a predator. I don't think we know yet whether predatory aggression actually occurs in humans, even those who are sociopathic.

Types of Defensive Aggression

In contrast to predatory aggression, defensive aggression is emotionally charged. Here, offensive action is imbued with the emotion of anger to create what is usually labeled "aggression." It is interesting and important to consider some of the other names given to this defensive reaction, such as *affective anger or aggression*, a term emphasizing the emotional component; *defensive rage*, which occurs in response to life-threatening situations; and *irritable anger or aggression*, which arises due to relatively small annoyances, rather than always in response to a serious threat. In regard to defensive rage, survivors often report that they lost conscious awareness while fighting for their lives; this experience is sometimes referred to as blind rage.

Defensive aggression follows a known pathway in the brain that I will detail in the coming pages. Before doing so, however, let me describe several different types of defensive aggression, which all follow this same basic pathway in the brain: intermale aggression, maternal aggression, sex-related aggression, fear-induced aggression, and irritable aggression. These types were suggested by psychologist Kenneth Moyer in 1976. These have remained useful and still appear in the literature today. Although all of these categories are useful, I'll primarily focus on fear-induced aggression and anger and irritable aggression and anger in this book, since these are the types that usually bring people into therapy.

Intermale Aggression

Intermale aggression takes place in many species of animals as males fight over access to females. The goal, of course, is to pass their genes on through sexual reproduction. Although these encounters can be fatal to one or both parties (think of two male elk whose horns have become locked together), they are usually ritualized to prevent serious injury. The battle is broken off once one of the antagonists demonstrates dominance over the other.

How about humans? Do men fight each other over access to women? Of course they do. Men attack each other with great regularity, sometimes fatally. On the other hand, humans have developed many ways to minimize these battles, probably the most important of which is the institution of marriage. That ring on a woman's finger clearly informs men not to go into battle over her. Still, it's likely that the brains of human males do have some deep evolutionary programming for intermale aggression.

Maternal Aggression

Maternal aggression is, in a sense, the female counterpart to intermale aggression. However, the battle here isn't for access to adult males; the purpose of maternal aggression is to protect offspring. A mother must on occasion fend off the attacks of various predators, sometimes including males of the same species who would kill her offspring in order to speed her return to reproductive readiness, as occurs among bears, lions, and other species. Females sometimes battle to the death to save their progeny.

As usual, the human picture is complicated. Human mothers' brains are certainly programmed to defend their children, but most fathers will also fight for the same cause. And as is often the case, civilization has played a major role in modifying basic instincts, so that adoptive parents and step-parents typically feel similarly protective. Most importantly, in many cultures the society itself has taken on the role of child protector, usually alleviating the need for mothers to physically defend their children.

That mention of step-parents reminds me how often I see blended families in counseling. Frequently the situation is that a new man has entered the scene after a woman with children has divorced her previous partner. Now the stepfather wants to be treated as an authority—as someone the children respect and obey—and comes across as rather harsh, at least to his newly acquired family. The kids protest and Mom ends up defending them, sometimes fiercely. Here's what I tell those stepdads: If you make a woman choose between you and her children, she will almost always choose her kids. This may be a slight exaggeration, but it speaks to the power of maternal brain wiring.

Sex-Related Aggression

Males of some species aggressively threaten or attack females during courtship. Again, most of this behavior is ritualized, but rape has been observed in geese and other animal species.

Human male acts of sexual aggression occur along a continuum ranging from mutually accepted playful aggression to violent rape. Sexual assault by human males has long been categorized by some writers as an act of power and control that actually has little to do with sexual desire. This assertion seems most viable when the sexual act is accompanied by sadistic brutality, including beating and torture.

Fear-Induced Aggression

When animals are in a situation where they face danger, they typically try to escape, freeze to avoid detection, or engage in submissive gestures—basically doing anything they can to avoid being attacked. But what if animals are cornered and none of these tactics works? When seriously threatened and unable to escape, animals often become enraged and attack out of desperation. This is fear-induced aggression.

Fear-induced aggression demonstrates that anger and fear are very closely related emotions. Their common bond is a perceived threat, which triggers a fight, flight, or freeze reaction in the brain. An organism's survival depends on its ability to select quickly and well among these options. Consequently, it is understandable that the pathways for fear and anger are clearly connected in the brain. Indeed, in terms of many threatening situations it may be wise to think of anger and fear as one combined emotional reaction. This may be particularly true with people who have been traumatized by past abuse. While these individuals often endure terrible fears that practically paralyze them, they are also capable of sudden and irrational acts of violence toward real or imagined threats. I'll discuss fear-induced aggression and anger in detail in chapter 6, Recognizing Unconscious Anger Activation.

Irritable Aggression

Have you ever seen an animal having a bad day? Sometimes it seems that my cat, Sarah, wakes up ornery and stays that way for hours. When she's in this mood she hisses at anything and everything. She even chases after her tail as if to punish it for following after her. I don't bother trying to be nice to her at those times; she'll have none of it. Even our dogs know not to mess with her on those days.

Irritable aggression is unlike most other forms of aggression because it is relatively nonspecific. Once you come under the sway of irritable aggression or anger, almost anything or anyone can become your target; it need not be someone or something that directly caused you pain or put you in danger. An example would be if your boss got on your case in the morning and set off an episode of irritable anger. You could very well bring that emotion home with you, so spouse and kids beware!

What triggers an outburst of irritable aggression? One cause is frustration, that vague term that most people use when things aren't going their way over a long period of time. Other causes include hunger, thirst, sleep problems, lack of social contact, physical pain, emotional pain, and worry. "Irritable aggression" is a broad term that covers a wide range of thoughts and behaviors. In one sense it's a catchall category that's too wide-ranging to be useful. But the great majority of people I see for anger and aggression problems come because of irritable anger. They realize that they get angry too often without good reason and that they take out their anger on the wrong people, at the wrong time, and for the wrong reason.

Switching On Defensive Aggression

Researchers have identified the pathways that the brain uses during episodes of defensive aggression and anger (Siegel 2005). Although the details are complicated, it is possible to outline a relatively straightforward description of these pathways. Here are the central components of the preconscious defensive anger system, which I'll elaborate upon throughout the book:

Sensory centers: Collect uninterpreted data from sensory organs.

Thalamus: Gathers and sends on emotionally relevant sensory information.

Medial amygdala: A center for emotional memory; becomes stimulated by possibly threatening information.

Medial hypothalamus: Controls autonomic functions that activate aggressive reactions.

Dorsolateral PAG: Triggers motor and autonomic nervous system action. (As a reminder, PAG stands for periaqueductal gray.)

Motor centers: Take defensive action when so directed.

The simplest possible route to an act of defensive aggression is as follows:

1. The medial amygdala (one of many nuclei clusters in the amygdala) is aroused by a possibly threatening stimulus.

2. It sends a message to the medial hypothalamus (one of several nuclei in the hypothalamus).

3. The message continues to the dorsolateral PAG, in the midbrain.

4. The PAG triggers motor and autonomic nervous system reactions, resulting in a defensive reaction.

As mentioned in chapter 1, the amygdala, which is part of the limbic system, is considered an essential and primary component in defensive aggressive actions. It is always involved. So is the hypothalamus, a tremendously important brain system that activates many of the body's endocrine glands. The PAG, although probably less studied than the amygdala and hypothalamus, must also be activated in a defensive aggressive reaction. If somehow the neural pathways connecting the PAG to the hypothalamus and amygdala were severed, you could not respond in this manner, no matter how threatening the danger.

You may wonder exactly how the amygdala receives danger signals. Is it directly connected with the sensory organs? It is, but only to one sensory organ—the nose, as indicated by the original name of the limbic system: the rhinencephalon. The root word is "rhino," which means "nose" in Latin. We acknowledge the power of our sense of smell with phrases like "the smell of danger" or "smelling a rat." So the amygdala can trigger defensive aggression directly in response to sensory information, but only in reaction to a bad odor.

Another brain structure is required to deal with information coming from the other sensory organs: the thalamus. It would be far too complicated to engage in a discussion of all the parts of the brain dealing with sensory information. (Remember that the entire occipital lobe, located in the back of the brain, is devoted to visual stimuli.) Rather than getting into those details, I'll just offer the insight that we usually see, hear, taste, touch, and smell what we're expecting to encounter. Furthermore, people primed to expect danger tend to seek it out both consciously and unconsciously. Our sensory organs are hardly neutral in this regard.

Based on this additional information, I can now expand on the brain's defensive anger and aggression system. Here's how it looks:

1. The sensory organs gather information about possible threats, and that information is processed in various regions of the brain.

2. The thalamus, located above the hypothalamus, gathers and organizes this information and transmits it to the amygdala.

3. The medial amygdala is aroused by a possibly threatening stimulus.

4. It sends a message to the medial hypothalamus.

5. The message continues to the dorsolateral PAG, in the midbrain.

6. The PAG triggers motor and autonomic nervous system reactions, resulting in a defensive reaction.

Now we're really getting somewhere. We have a description of the core pathway the brain uses whenever it fires up defensive anger and aggression. But something is missing. There has been no mention of conscious awareness. Not that conscious awareness is required; you can react defensively without it, at least in the initial stages, and particularly the activation stage (as I'll detail in chapter 6). Nevertheless, if you are to change your mind-set and actions, we can't stop here. We need to continue into the realm of conscious awareness so we can eventually get to conscious choice.

Two regions of the brain must be added to the process outlined above to accomplish this task. The first is the frontal cortex, specifically the orbitofrontal and dorsolateral prefrontal cortex, which, as mentioned in chapter 1, give you the ability to control your impulses, prioritize behavior, and understand how your actions will be received by others. The second region is the hippocampus, the component of the limbic system that helps you keep problems in perspective and allows you to distinguish between threatening and nonthreatening situations.

Now comes the complicated part. The brain always initially handles threats without necessarily invoking consciousness; it only sometimes adds a conscious component. That means there are actually two overlapping pathways to defensive aggression. The second pathway looks like this:

1. The sensory organs gather information about possible threats, and that information is processed in various regions of the brain.

2. The thalamus gathers and organizes this information and transmits it to the amygdala.

3. The medial amygdala is aroused by a possibly threatening stimulus.

4. It sends a message to the medial hypothalamus.

5. The message continues to the dorsolateral PAG, in the midbrain.

6. The thalamus, amygdala, and PAG all send information to the frontal cortex and hippocampus. This information is processed and a conscious decision is made about how to respond.

7. If a show of defensive aggression is warranted, the PAG triggers motor and autonomic nervous system reactions, resulting in a defensive reaction.

It probably takes two to three seconds for the brain to do all of this conscious work. That doesn't sound like much, but it is, especially when compared to the less than half a second it takes to activate the system without conscious awareness. Basically, this means that angry defensive reactions are always ahead of the conscious ability to stop them. That two- to three-second differential is a big reason why people act before they think.

However, you can learn to forestall the unconscious reaction until you've had a chance to utilize the second pathway. And, better yet, you can increase the time between your initial, primarily unconscious angry defensive reaction and your chosen behavior. When you are first learning to control your anger, three seconds can make a big difference. And as you get better at controlling your anger, you'll be able to increase the time between your impulses and your actions.

Switching Off Defensive and Predatory Aggression

Improving your ability to switch off the defensive aggression response is the key to developing anger management skills, particularly in situations where you tend to act before you think. In contrast to switching on the defensive aggression mechanism, switching it off is essentially a conscious operation. Both the frontal cortex and the hippocampus play key roles in deactivating the system. The frontal cortex sends particularly strong messages to quiet down to the thalamus, which transmits them to the hypothalamus. Meanwhile, the hippocampus works more indirectly, sending messages to another region of the limbic system, the *septum*, to shut down predatory aggression, which in turn directs the hypothalamus to shut down the defensive aggressive reaction. If this all works as it should, essentially your brain has initially reacted to a possible threat, prepared to respond to it, and then recognized that there was no real danger and therefore cut back its response before doing anything physical. Here's an overview of the brain systems involved in shutting down defensive anger to shut down defensive and predatory aggression:

Orbitofrontal cortex: Can apply impulse control to slow down or stop an initial angry impulse.

Dorsolateral prefrontal cortex: Prioritizes emotionally influenced behavior to allow greater ability to choose appropriate action.

Hippocampus: Sends information to the septum to cease defensive aggression and shut down predatory aggression.

Septum: Relays information to the hypothalamus to cease defensive aggression and shut down predatory aggression.

Thalamus: Receives messages to shut down defensive aggression from the frontal cortex.

Hypothalamus: Shuts down the defensive aggression system when so directed.

One note about the septum: Researchers can shock the septum of animals into inactivity. The result, called septic rage, is an uncontrollably violent response that continues until the function of the septum is restored. This demonstrates that the septum plays a major role in the inhibition of aggression.

In order to help make the brain mechanics of predatory and defensive aggression more comprehensible, I omitted discussion of other brain areas associated with both the activation and the suppression of either predatory or defensive aggression. One such region is the bed nucleus of the stria terminalis, which receives input from the amygdala and sends information to the hypothalamus, thus facilitating defensive aggression. Another is the substantia innominata, which serves to increase predatory attack. In addition, I've understated the amount of information going in all directions during aggressive encounters. For example, the amygdala has many fibers, or axons, sending messages to the frontal cortex, and these probably have the effect of increasing the probability of aggression. The frontal cortex, in the meantime, has its own direct links with the amygdala, although fewer in number. This implies that the amygdala may have a stronger immediate effect on the frontal cortex than vice versa. I also haven't addressed how the neurotransmitters serotonin and dopamine affect defensive aggression, but I'll discuss this later in the book. For now, I believe the descriptions above suffice to give an overview of how the angry brain works—an understanding that will provide an important foundation as you begin to change how your brain deals with anger.

The Six Stages of Well-Handled Anger

Let's revisit the six-stage model of emotional processing I described in chapter 2. Here it is again to refresh your memory:

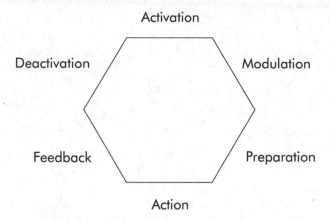

Figure 7. The six stages of an anger episode.

As discussed, when you handle an emotion well, you travel through these six stages effectively and efficiently. On the other hand, it's possible to handle any or all of these stages poorly, so that instead of you resolving whatever issue or opportunity triggered the emotion, the situation remains unsettled or even gets worse.

In the remainder of this chapter, I'll use an example of a typical anger scenario to illustrate how it might be handled well, and then how it might be handled poorly. In this example, Melvin is married to Sarah, a home decorator and store manager. She's just gotten home and has exciting news. Her boss has offered her the job of regional manager for the entire state. It's a huge career opportunity and also means a big raise in salary. If Melvin handles his anger well, his anger episode might look like this:

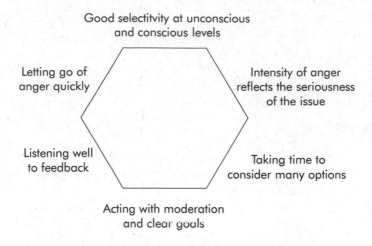

Figure 8. The six stages of well-handled anger.

Stage 1: Well-Handled Anger Activation

Melvin should be happy for Sarah, right? And he does feel some happiness for her, knowing how proud and excited she feels. Plus, the extra money will help with their budget. But Melvin quickly becomes aware that something negative is going on in his body. He notices that his jaw has clamped down so hard that it's almost painful to speak. From past experience Melvin recognizes that this physical event is his personal anger cue; his tight jaw means he's angry but doesn't want to say what he's thinking. As his first step in handling anger well, Melvin knows his anger well enough to notice its appearance, even when half hidden. Also note that Melvin didn't consciously choose to feel angry. As often happens at the activation stage, his anger developed instantaneously and unbidden, at the preconscious level. But now that his anger has announced its presence, it's up to Melvin to handle it well.

Stage 2: Well-Handled Anger Modulation

Melvin does something really smart. He takes a brief time-out. He says, "Honey, would you like a cup of coffee? It will only take a couple minutes to make it." That break allows him to think about his situation and prevents him from blurting out something he'll immediately regret. Basically, Melvin needs to take an intensity reading. Is he just a little bit mad, moderately angry, or really irate? If he's been taking anger management classes, Melvin might even rate his anger on a scale from 0 to 10. While that's a good refinement, what's most important at this stage is that Melvin get a sense of how upset he is so he can try to respond with a proportionate level of intensity. Melvin discovers that his anger is somewhere in the middle range.

Stage 3: Well-Handled Anger Preparation

"Think, think, think" should be the motto for this stage of the emotion cycle. Melvin considers his options, which in theory could range from saying nothing to going berserk. If Melvin's anger were at a low level, he would just let it go and celebrate with Sarah. But that would mean stuffing his anger, which doesn't work well with anger at the moderate and higher levels, so he decides he'd better say something. The issue he has to resolve is how he can share his anger without getting into an argument and ruining the rest of their day. He decides to try to de-emphasize his anger in the hope that this will help Sarah consider his issues nondefensively. He decides to tell Sarah that he's basically very happy for her, but that he does have one concern.

Stage 4: Well-Handled Anger Action

Melvin brings their coffee into the dining area. He tells Sarah that he's happy for her and proud of her. Then he tells her that one thing is bothering him, and he needs to talk about it. He says, "Maybe I'm being selfish, but I'm thinking about how much less time the kids and I will have with you if you take this job. Plus, you haven't mentioned how much you'll have to travel. That's the reason the last regional manager quit, remember?" To his relief, Sarah tells him that this was the first thing she discussed with her boss and that he agreed that she would only have to go on the road one week a month, rather than traveling every week as her predecessor did. Sarah says that she too is concerned about having less time with the family. Sarah and Melvin agree that they'll need to think creatively about ways they can have enough time together.

Stage 5: Well-Handled Anger Feedback

At this point, Melvin needs to ask himself whether he's still angry or upset. If not, then he can move on to the deactivation stage. But if he's unsatisfied with the results of their conversation, this would be the time to deal with those feelings. So Melvin scans his body and mind and discovers that he's a little anxious. He recognizes that this emotion is fairly normal for him. He's never liked change very much—even good changes. However, he's not angry anymore, and that's a relief.

Feedback comes from Sarah, too. She tells him that she's glad he brought up his concerns, because she wants both of them to be happy about her promotion. Sarah's positive feedback helps Melvin feel okay about how he responded and what he said.

Stage 6: Well-Handled Anger Deactivation

Melvin could keep fretting about Sarah's promotion. Fortunately, he's able to put his worries aside so that he and Sarah can celebrate her promotion. Chances are, he'll need to talk with her about his concerns again later. In real life, people seldom resolve their concerns and conflicts in one easy discussion. But for the time being, Melvin is able to let go of feeling threatened. His frontal cortex and hippocampus turn off the defensive aggression response. Soon his blood pressure returns to normal and his entire body relaxes.

The Six Stages of Poorly Handled Anger

Six stages, six opportunities for fallible human beings to screw up the way they manage their anger. And because anger is a troublesome emotion that most people find hard to handle, almost everyone will have some difficulty traversing all six stages with grace and dignity. To give you an idea of what goes wrong and why, we'll look at that same situation and see how Melvin might mishandle his anger at each stage. But first, here's the model again, this time showing the typical pitfalls that lead to poorly handled anger:

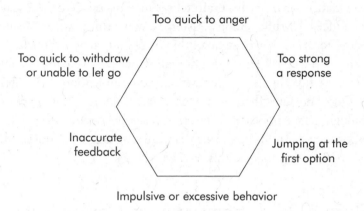

Figure 9. The six stages of poorly handled anger.

Stage 1: Poorly Handled Anger Activation

Sarah walks in the door smiling. "Oh, crap," thinks Melvin. "Something's up." Sarah hasn't even said a word yet, and Melvin is already feeling threatened. His anxiety level rises. And because his anxiety triggers a fight-or-flight reaction, Melvin is immediately ready for an argument. In fact, because his amygdala immediately and automatically activated his nervous system, at the preconscious level he's already in a fight without even knowing it. If Melvin has an anger problem, this probably isn't the first time this has happened to him; rather, his anger probably often gets triggered automatically, before he knows what's going on. At this point, it really won't matter much what Sarah says. Melvin's brain is primed to gather only negative information that will justify his anger and aggression.

Stage 2: Poorly Handled Anger Modulation

Sarah gets one partial sentence out of her mouth: "My boss just offered me a promotion and..." Melvin doesn't need to hear anything more. That's enough bad news for Melvin's anger-ready brain to confirm his worst fears. "Danger, danger, danger," his brain tells him. This is a 10 on the scale of 0 to 10—a life(style)-threatening disaster. To make things worse, his intense emotional reaction is accompanied by an old automatic thought: "She's doing this to hurt me." That thought really infuriates Melvin—so much so that he can't take in the rest of Sarah's communication. His automatic thought also indicates that his hippocampus is doing a biased job of sorting through his memories of scenes that resemble this one to help inform his response. It's as if his hippocampus were scanning all of the similar old pictures but pausing to look only at the bad ones.

Stage 3: Poorly Handled Anger Preparation

The amygdala has more fibers, or axons, sending messages to the frontal cortex than the frontal cortex has to the amygdala. That means the frontal lobes, the center for executive control, can be overwhelmed by a highly activated amygdala. When that happens, you can say good-bye to objective reasoning, keeping things in perspective, and impulse control and say hello to outrage!

In the midst of an anger episode, angry people don't really plan. They seldom take a time-out to consider their options. Instead, they lunge at some immediate action they can take on behalf of their anger. What little planning they do is heavily weighted toward aggressive behaviors. Melvin's "plan," if you can call it that, is to attack immediately by insisting that Sarah call her boss and decline the promotion.

Stage 4: Poorly Handled Anger Action

Melvin jumps in. He interrupts Sarah before she can finish her first sentence. He shouts, swears, and makes demands. He treats her like she's his enemy instead of his partner in life. Nothing she says makes a difference, which isn't surprising, as Melvin isn't really listening to her at all. He's tuning in to and reacting to his anger, and the result is verbal aggression. Like a forest fire, his anger feeds on itself.

Even at this stage, Melvin could salvage the situation if he would just step outside of himself and see what he's doing. If he could see how ridiculously he's behaving, perhaps he could regain control. Although that's very difficult to do at this stage, I've heard many stories from very angry clients who managed to curtail their aggression, just as a sudden rain can put out a forest fire.

What if I added that Melvin has been having problems with depression? That would suggest that one reason he can't control his anger is low serotonin levels in his brain. Low serotonin is associated with impulsive aggression.

Stage 5: Poorly Handled Anger Feedback

Sarah is crying. She feels hurt, shamed, and attacked. Her good news has turned into a disaster. She flees to the bedroom, telling Melvin to leave her alone. That is clearly negative feedback, and it should tell Melvin to stop what he's doing because it isn't having the desired result. Unfortunately, Melvin is too riled up to get the message. He still wants to argue. So he stomps into the bedroom after her. His internal feedback system is still saying, "I'm right. I just have to keep yelling and make her listen." Now his anger is becoming abusive. He's only one step away from physical violence.

Melvin has another problem at the feedback stage. He's never been good at putting himself in another person's shoes. His poor empathy translates into not being able to feel Sarah's anguish. It's not that Melvin doesn't care about her feelings; it's more that he's unable to experience them, especially when he's angry.

It's possible that in a couple of hours Melvin will feel like a fool and truly regret how he behaved. That's important internal negative feedback and hopefully will help him change how he reacts in the future. But even if that were to happen, his negative feedback would come too late. He's already done a lot of unnecessary damage to his relationship.

Stage 6: Poorly Handled Anger Deactivation

Poor Melvin. Not only does he have problems with his amygdala, hippocampus, frontal cortex, and serotonin system that predispose him to anger, but also his anterior cingulate, his caudate nucleus, or both don't work very well. These two areas help the brain shift gears. When they function poorly, a person has difficulty letting go of whatever is troublesome. It's like having a car stuck in reverse or neutral—either way, you can't go forward with your life. So Melvin can't deactivate his anger in regard to this situation. He thinks about it repeatedly, and every time he does so he makes himself angry all over again. Days later he still doesn't know the whole story. He's stuck on "How can you do this to me and the kids?" and Sarah refuses to discuss the matter with him. He's more than ready to take up the fight again, but because Sarah won't argue with him, he takes his complaints elsewhere, to family and friends, until they too are sick of his attitude.

Summary

Fortunately, few people have problems at as many stages of an anger episode as Melvin does. Wherever your problems lie, the good news is that it's possible to become less angry and gain better control over your anger at each of the six stages. This book will help you do just that. But before we proceed, it's critical to have a good understanding of what might cause someone to have a brain tilted toward anger. That's the topic of the next chapter.

Chapter 4

The Causes of an Angry Brain

We've just looked at how poorly handled anger might play out. Now I need to address another concern—indeed, the one that might be why you've chosen to read this book. The critical question is this: how does a person develop an angry brain? The answer to this question, as you probably expect by now, is complicated. Recall that when I say a person has an angry brain, I mean that person tends to get angry too often, become too excited when angry, plan poorly and act badly when upset, have trouble letting go of anger, or some combination or all of the above.

It would probably be most accurate to title this chapter "The Many Factors That Can Increase the Risk for Getting Too Angry." I'll be describing several ways that a person can develop habitual patterns of anger and aggression. The main point, though, is that the brain itself can and does become acclimated to anger. When it does, you'll start becoming more angry more rapidly, you'll stay angry longer, and you'll be more likely to take your anger into the realm of verbal or physical aggression.

The Anger Superhighway

Think of anger as if it were a road. Some people's anger road is a virtually deserted, weed-covered gravel path. For others it's a fairly busy side street. And for some it's a superhighway. They go way too fast, their anger accelerating from 0 to 100 miles per hour in seconds. Plus, they make impulsive decisions that often cause them to wreck their vehicle. As you can imagine, they seldom hesitate to give other drivers a piece of their mind. And they drive so fast and hard that they often miss their exit ramp.

Actually, there's a better analogy. Rather than a superhighway, their anger is a toll road because they pay a heavy price for it. So how do people get on that anger toll road? In this chapter, we'll examine some of the ways. However, please note that there is no single neurological cause for anger and aggression. Rather, there are many different factors to consider. Just as a driver can get onto a toll road at many entrances, people can develop angry brains via many different routes. Here are the most common causes of anger and aggression:

- Frustration

- Too much stress

- Physical or emotional trauma

- Alcohol and drug abuse

- Excessive hormone release

- Problems with neurotransmitters

- Genetic personality factors that promote anger

- Families and cultures that promote anger and aggression

- Brain malfunctions

While one person might be affected by only one or two of these causes, another person may have several factors contributing to an angry brain. People with several different anger-generating brain pathways are likely to have more frequent and intense anger problems because their anger gets triggered in many ways. In addition, causes of anger may feed each other.

For example, someone with a history of frontal lobe damage who is going through a period of great stress will find that the stress makes it harder to think and that thinking problems due to frontal lobe damage add to the stress.

Nobody Has a Perfect Brain

If only I had a perfect brain. Then I'd never wake up anxious without cause. I wouldn't exaggerate problems. I wouldn't get irritable. I'd always remember to breathe deeply to help myself stay calm. I wouldn't lose my temper even when provoked. But I don't have a perfect brain. Nobody has a perfect brain. That means we are all, to a certain extent, vulnerable to bouts of excessive anger, verbal aggression, and even physical aggression.

The brain learns by the principle of association. This means that any two things that happen at the same time or in quick succession can become linked in our minds. Perhaps you've heard of Pavlov's dogs. They learned to so closely associate the ringing of a bell with receiving food that they salivated as soon as the bell rang. Given our intellectual capacity, we humans are probably even better than canines at learning associations. We have the ability to associate essentially anything with anything else as long as the two events happen almost simultaneously. That's normally a quite beneficial trait. Our survival depends upon making appropriate associations; for instance, a car careening toward you should be associated with a possible threat to your life.

Unfortunately, learned associations aren't always helpful. For proof of this, just go to a casino and watch people making all kinds of ridiculous gestures. They believe these motions will bring them luck. Quite possibly, they happened to win big at a moment when by chance they were swinging their arms through the air, clapping their hands, or scratching their head. Learned associations are strengthened when a person is having a strong emotional experience, and for those folks at the casino, their brain needed only one pairing to conclude that winning big was caused by arm swinging, clapping, or scratching. Misassociations like this are accurately labeled superstitions. Unfortunately it isn't easy to break associations. Unlearning them takes more—usually far more—conscious effort than learning them.

It's easy to develop learned but inaccurate associations that lead to irrational anger. For example, you may have learned to associate "Honey, let's talk" with the thought "Oh, great, here comes another lecture about what I'm doing wrong." If so, you'll get angry every time you hear that phrase, even if your partner is just as likely to use it to initiate a positive conversation. It's possible that you actually linked criticism with this phrase long ago when a parent or previous partner used it. But because you still associate "Let's talk" with criticism, you bristle whenever you hear it.

We tend to think the brain loyally paints accurate pictures of reality. But the primary purpose of the brain is to ensure our survival so we can pass our genes along to the next generation. Consciousness can help us survive, to be sure. But sometimes our physical and emotional survival might better be served when the brain blocks complete awareness. One example is that most people can't remember much about what happened to them during traumatic events like automobile accidents or muggings. Blocking full anticipation of the inevitability of death is another way the brain protects us by limiting our conscious awareness. There are many other ways in which the human brain distorts accurate awareness. It tends to do all of the following at least occasionally:

- Exaggerate

- Deny

- Minimize

- Misjudge

- Issue false alarms

- Hide things from consciousness

- Ignore facts

- Leap to inaccurate conclusions

- Dissociate

- Oversimplify

- Confuse cause and effect

- Refuse to learn

So you might find yourself on the anger toll road because your brain sometimes makes mistakes. It's likely that the worst mistake occurs when your brain erroneously perceives a threat. It shouts, "*Danger! Danger!*" when there is no danger. Your job is to catch these mistakes and correct them whenever you can. That means taking the first exit off the anger toll road by doing things like replacing an anger-provoking thought with a calming one, taking a time-out, or choosing to look for the good instead of the bad in people. It's also important to develop a support group of friends, family, and associates who aren't afraid to tell you when your brain is going off track.

Factors That May Cause an Angry Brain

So it's natural for the human brain to make mistakes—and even to distort reality. Clearly that can send us off track in many different directions. Now let's take a close look at how people might become angry when the brain distorts reality.

Frustration

I hear one word over and over again when I ask people why they are angry: "frustration." This is a shorthand way of saying that troublesome reality has struck again. The lawnmower broke down. Your kids didn't do their chores. Your partner came home late. Your boss has unreasonable expectations. First one thing goes wrong and then another, and suddenly you're on the anger toll road, even though you'd planned to take a different route.

This aggravated feeling is virtually universal. Everyone becomes frustrated at least occasionally. So just because you occasionally become frustrated doesn't mean you're destined to have a permanently angry brain. You can work on calming your brain if you find yourself feeling frustrated quite frequently or if when you get frustrated you say and do things you later regret.

Too Much Stress

I recently had six members of one of my anger groups take a standardized stress test. A high score on this test was listed as anything above 300 points. Two of the angry men in that group scored over 450 points, and a third scored a whopping 758. Even worse, they've been like this for months or years. Their lives are full of long-term stressors like joblessness, having children with serious medical conditions, marital separations, and legal troubles. These three guys are heading toward nervous breakdowns, accidents, illness, or strokes. Human bodies are simply not designed to handle that much stress for an extended period. Is it any wonder that they report feeling anxious and irritable all the time?

Stress triggers the fight-or-flight reaction. But fight or flight is meant to be a short-term reaction to danger. And in the short term, it's helpful, not damaging, that stress hormones are released in massive amounts, breathing rate accelerates, heart rate soars, attention gets focused on the danger, and muscles get ready for action. But in the long term, these and other effects of stress do a lot of damage to your body and brain.

Excessive stress is a major reason people develop and maintain an angry brain. That's why breathing exercises, relaxation training, and meditation work so well to help people become less angry. These techniques help people relieve the feeling of stress. Metaphorically speaking, lowering your stress means getting off the anger toll road and taking a quieter path.

Trauma

A traumatized brain is one that has been massively altered. This can happen when a person either witnesses or is the victim of an extremely violent or life-threatening situation. Beatings, sexual abuse, attempted murder, or the threat of these things can change a person's brain—possibly forever. Although we usually think of trauma victims as being easily terrified, avoidant, and generally fearful, they may also develop a hair-trigger defensive system, distrust of others, paranoia, and an irritable demeanor.

A critical point in regard to anger management is that the hippocampus is one part of the brain that's extremely vulnerable to stress hormones. Extended exposure to these stress hormones (glucocorticoids) can damage the hippocampus. That damage limits a person's ability to put things into proper perspective. Also, remember that the hippocampus is a key player in turning off the aggression process in animals and probably humans as well. A damaged hippocampus could potentially disrupt this mechanism.

Alcohol and Drug Abuse

Among causes of anger, substance abuse is a big one. About half of the people I and my wife, Pat, see for anger, aggression, and domestic abuse committed their aggressive acts while under the immediate influence of alcohol or drugs. That doesn't include the people who weren't high or impaired at the moment but whose addictive lifestyle made them more hostile, defensive, or paranoid. These substances are truly mood altering both short-term and long-term. Unfortunately, all too often the direction of mood change is from mellow to nasty, even when the opposite effect is intended.

Mood-altering substances primarily attack the brain's judgment centers in the frontal cortex. At the extreme, people black out completely. True, they may not do anything horrible in this state; nothing about substance use is 100 percent predictable. But once intoxicated people pass the threshold for aggression, it becomes more likely that they will do so again and again.

Staying sober is the single most important thing many people can do to lessen their angry mood and behavior. That calls for a strong commitment of exactly the kind that produces real brain change—a topic we'll look at in detail later in the book.

Hormone Imbalances

Hormones are naturally occurring chemicals that are released into the bloodstream when the brain directs specific organs to do so. Examples are adrenaline; insulin; the previously mentioned glucocorticoids, which are related to the stress response; and sex-related hormones such as testosterone, estrogen, and progesterone.

Some hormones can have a profound effect on mood. For example, consider hypoglycemia, a condition caused by an immediate lack of blood sugar. Many people who have suffered a bout of hypoglycemia can attest that it causes irritability, confusion, and aggressiveness. What astonishes me is how someone undergoing a hypoglycemic attack quits being so angry and grumpy within minutes once the condition is corrected with a glass of orange juice.

A key point here is that hormone levels wax and wane in our bodies. So if someone suffers from rapid and inexplicable bouts of anger, it might relate to a hormone imbalance. If that sounds like your situation, you probably should make an appointment with your doctor to discuss the matter.

Testosterone has often been associated with male anger and aggression. Certainly, males of many species are more aggressive than females. And male teenagers, whose testosterone levels are the highest they will ever be, do tend to get into a lot of trouble. So it would seem pretty obvious that the more testosterone secreted by the testes, the angrier and more aggressive a man will become. Although some studies do seem to support this idea, the majority of the evidence doesn't appear to indicate that testosterone level is a very good predictor for anger or aggression. The correlations between testosterone level and behavior are relatively low, meaning that testosterone levels don't explain much about why some men are more aggressive than others (Sapolsky 2005). Additionally, sometimes the aggression-testosterone link seems reversed from what you might expect. For instance, a man's testosterone level will rise when he resoundingly wins a sporting contest and will be lowered if he loses, or even if he squeaks by with a narrow victory (Sapolsky 2005). It's not that a high testosterone level promoted victory; rather, victory promoted a rise in testosterone.

What about estrogen and progesterone? Women are more likely to become aggressive just before and during menstruation, when there is less estrogen in proportion to progesterone (Sapolsky 2005). But again the relationship is a fairly weak one. Most importantly, for both men and women it appears that expectations about what will happen are at least as important as actual hormonal changes. At this point in time, it's safest to conclude that sex-linked hormones have some influence on aggressive behavior, but for most people they aren't the most important factor.

Problems with Neurotransmitters

Neurotransmitters are chemicals created within the brain (and some-times elsewhere) that *transmit* information between *neurons*, which is how they received their name. They travel through the tiny space between neurons, the synaptic gap, allowing the electrical and chemical brain sys-tem to transfer information from the sending portion of one neuron (the axon) to the receiving part of the next neuron (the dendrites) in the chain. Each neurotransmitter has special physical characteristics that match the shape of receptor sites on the receiving neuron, much as a key fits into a lock. This fine-tuning of brain networks is meant to ensure that correct and exact messages eventually go to neurons that activate everything from breathing to reading a book.

One of the main tasks of the neurotransmitter serotonin is to help inhibit impulses. In other words, when you get angry, you need serotonin to kick in and help you stop and think before you say or do something you may regret. People with low serotonin levels have a well-documented ten-dency toward anger, irritability, and impulsive aggression. Biochemical depression is also strongly associated with low serotonin. That's why depressed individuals frequently seem grouchy, short-tempered, and even suicidal. It's important to note that many men in American society have a distinct aversion to admitting they're having problems with depression. They also tend to stubbornly resist taking antidepressants, no matter how appropriate this would be. These men will admit that they have serious anger problems while refusing to take a pill or two every day that might help them feel less irritable.

I've previously noted that the neurotransmitter GABA suppresses defensive rage. Additionally, GABA serves as the brain's most general calming neurotransmitter, the complement to glutamate, which is the brain's general activating neurotransmitter. Some people take GABA sup-plements to help them stay calm; however, the effectiveness of this nutri-tional supplement for anger control has not been documented.

Excessive anger and aggression are sometimes associated with the neurotransmitters dopamine and norepinephrine. However, the relation-ships here are quite complex. For example, we need dopamine in the fron-tal lobes to help us think of alternatives to aggression. But when the brain is forced to make too much dopamine, for example through repeated use of cocaine, the entire inhibitory system tends to break down.

Genetic Personality Factors That Promote Anger

No single "anger gene" has been discovered. However, some people are born with a combination of genetic characteristics that increase their likelihood of developing anger and aggression problems. These may include a low tolerance for frustration, hypersensitivity to sounds or touch, inflexible patterns of thinking, a tendency toward impulsivity, or low sensitivity to negative feedback (which means that punishment has little effect). If you have some of these traits, don't be discouraged. These characteristics don't make anger problems inevitable. They simply increase the odds. What matters most, in terms of genetic predispositions toward any behavior, is how strongly one's family and society encourage or discourage expression of that behavior.

Here's an excellent example: Scientists discovered about a decade ago that one variant of a particular gene was associated with aggression. More specifically, men who had a relatively rare version of the MAO (monoamine oxidase) gene, labeled MAOA (monoamine oxidase A), were frequently arrested and imprisoned. But then researchers made a remarkable discovery. The MAOA gene caused trouble only for men who had been raised in abusive homes (Dobbs 2009). It didn't matter whether they possessed the MAOA variant when they were raised in nonabusive homes. In fact, among men who had been raised in nonabusive conditions, this same gene (MAOA) actually lessened the risk of aggression compared to men with the standard MAO gene. It turns out that this gene is one of a category of genes sometimes called "orchid genes" because only when children are nurtured and treated well do they blossom beautifully.

Families and Cultures That Promote Anger and Aggression

This brings up a very important point. The human brain is a social brain. It's designed to help us survive in group settings—originally families and groups focused on raising children or hunting, and more recently cities, states, and work settings. Your brain is designed to learn about and adapt to the environment in which you live.

Children live in awe of their parents. That word "awe" implies that they both fear and worship their parents. Naturally, then, parental modeling sets the norm for adult behavior. Unfortunately, this sense of awe often translates into "My mom yelled, my dad threw things, and now I do both."

Too many children are raised in environments that promote anger and aggression. Sometimes that means growing up with a physically abusive parent. Anger is also promoted by highly shaming verbal abuse, such as "You are the dumbest kid I've ever seen. I'm ashamed to call you my son." Indeed, domestic abuse researcher Donald Dutton says that shaming of a male child by his father is the single strongest contributor toward that boy becoming a man who physically attacks women (Dutton 1998).

Nobody is doomed to repeat history. Even my most angry clients often tell me how much they want to be better parents to their kids than their parents were to them. But breaking the habits of a lifetime doesn't come easy. These men and women must work daily to speak gently and demonstrate their love and respect for their children.

Families aren't the only social source of anger and aggression. Every society sets guidelines, norms, and rules about when it's okay to get angry: with whom, under what circumstances, and so on. All you need to do is watch Sunday football to see how aggression has been packaged into an acceptable form in which a city's team symbolically goes to war with another city's team in an effort to establish dominance. This mostly symbolic aggression definitely saves lives. How would you like to live in a country where Detroit's standing army might go to war with Chicago's?

There's no question that the United States and many other countries have increasingly frowned upon individual displays of anger and aggression. Laws prohibiting acts of domestic violence, school bullying, child beating, and workplace violence are obvious indicators of this stance. So is the preference for dealing with an obnoxious neighbor by threatening legal action, as opposed to showing up at the neighbor's house with shotgun in hand. The probable underlying dynamic here is that larger societies must take formal steps to prohibit overt acts of violence because they cannot rely on informal controls to limit aggression. Practically speaking, it means there's an entire industry of counselors like me earning a living by helping people learn how to curb their anger and aggression in order to stay out of jail and maintain their relationships.

There is, however, a troubling countertrend that seems to be increasing the level of anger and aggression in the United States: an excessively angry and competitive climate in which politicians, talk show hosts, and average citizens willingly engage in savagely attacking each other. This take-no-prisoners attitude may be a temporary phenomenon. If not, it could reverse the long-term movement away from physical violence as the increasing level of verbal aggression starts spilling over into physical attacks.

Brain Malfunctions

As mentioned, nobody has a perfect brain. Unfortunately, some types of brain malfunctions greatly increase the risk for excessive anger and aggression. A person may be born with these problems, or problems may arise later as a result of brain damage due to injury or disease.

MINIMAL OR DIFFUSE BRAIN DAMAGE

The first type of damage I'll mention is actually the hardest to identify. It's called minimal or diffuse brain damage. Here's an example: Years ago I was a social worker at a hospital when I was asked to check on a fifteen-year-old girl, Julie, who had been in an automobile accident. Julie had been in the hospital for a few days recovering from her physical injuries. Because she'd hit her head on the dashboard, she was also subjected to a brain scan, which came back normal. Her family was quite upset because the doctors had pronounced Julie to be fit, healthy, and undamaged from the accident and were ready to send her home. And Julie did seem to be speaking and acting fine. But her parents insisted that something was wrong—that she was still acting oddly. "This isn't the real Julie," they kept repeating. They were especially worried because, once back at home, Julie got angry frequently, didn't listen to what they were saying, and generally acted far more oppositionally than she had before. They said that she had always been a happy child and easy to live with, but now she seemed generally sullen and sad.

I followed this family for several years. During that time Julie never regained her former happy disposition. She remained grouchy and moody. She picked fights with her family and friends. Her personality had changed permanently for the worse. Nevertheless, a brain scan she underwent several years later still failed to reveal any damage.

Who knows how many people suffer from this kind of "minimal" brain damage? Quite possibly, improved brain scanning tools will one day reveal more subtle levels of brain damage than we can currently detect. They may show that certain individuals have a bit of damage at several places in the brain. It could be that whereas damage at any one of these sites wouldn't cause significant problems alone, together they might increase affected individuals' aggressiveness and make it harder for them to inhibit their anger, anticipate negative consequences of their actions, respond empathically, or cope with conflicts verbally instead of physically. If we are eventually able to detect such subtle and diffuse damage, hopefully that will allow us to help people in this situation.

FRONTAL LOBE MALFUNCTION

Frontal lobe malfunctions are a major source of anger problems. People with frontal lobe malfunctions may have trouble concentrating, thinking problems through, and, most importantly, slowing down their angry reactions to perceived threats. You may recall that the frontal cortex (specifically, the prefrontal cortex, at the front of the front of the brain) is the area most needed for control of immediate impulses. It's here that people consciously choose not to give in to the urge to play, get drunk, or put off doing a difficult job. This skill, called *impulse delay* or *impulse inhibition*, hopefully leads to a bigger payoff later. But deferred gratification works only if you have the ability to put off immediate gratification, visualize long-term gains from doing so, and apply long-term effort to creating those rewards that develop more slowly. People with ineffective frontal lobes have trouble with all three of these skills: They are poor at initial impulse control; they can't really imagine waiting around minutes, hours, days, weeks, or years for a reward; and they lack the organizational skills to carry out long-term plans.

What does this have to do with anger and aggression? Impulse inhibition is essential for anger management. My clients often report that they said something in anger without thinking. More frequently, though, they do think about it and realize they should hold their tongue. But they go ahead with the sarcastic remark, cuss word, or insult anyway because their impulse control mechanisms aren't strong enough to contain their emotion.

Here's an analogy: Once a year I buy a load of corn for my horse, Lakota. The corn comes in sacks that range from about 60 to 120 pounds. Now, I'm small, old, and not terribly strong. I can carry a 60-pounder decently, but I struggle with the 90-pound sacks, and on a bad day I simply cannot lift the 120-pounders. Meanwhile, the forty-five-year-old, six-foot-two, hardworking farmer who sells me the corn is grabbing one sack with each hand and carrying them easily into the shed. In terms of impulse control, someone with frontal lobe difficulties is like me with the corn sacks, able to handle a small impulse but not able to control larger ones.

Imagine a child with less-than-perfect frontal lobe development. (This means most kids, since the frontal lobes continue to develop until people are in their midtwenties.) That child may be able to withhold making an angry remark after becoming a little upset over a minor issue, such as being told that TV time will be over in fifteen minutes. But shortly thereafter, when Mom or Dad announces it really is time to turn the television off— just a few minutes before the show ends—you can say good-bye to impulse control and anger management. The preliminary warning was only a 60-pound sack. The real deal was a 120-pounder, too heavy to carry.

This discussion raises an important question: Can people with frontal lobe deficits develop more strength in the area of impulse management? I could certainly work up to being able to carry those 120-pound sacks. It would take commitment and engaging in challenging weight training, but that goal is within the range of my genetically determined lifting capacity. Likewise, I think people with frontal lobe problems can set and achieve a goal of developing better-than-average impulse control and anger management skills. Why settle for less? I've seen kids do this over time, and I've spoken with many children and adults who have developed positive routines for impulse control. The two key elements, just as in my situation, are making a commitment and practicing a specific set of skills regularly.

Some people with frontal lobe irregularities, especially children, are diagnosed with attention deficit/hyperactivity disorder (ADHD). This tends to occur because they have difficulty concentrating and staying on task. In fact, ADHD appears to be primarily a massive dysregulation that applies from the prefrontal cortex all the way to the cerebellum. The link between anger, aggression, and ADHD arises because people with that condition have more difficulty containing their angry impulses. But I think it's important to mention another connection that has a bearing here. I once asked a reading specialist named Brenda who worked in my building whether she agreed with the idea that kids with ADHD often lose their temper. She became upset at the question and said, "Who wouldn't get angry when you live in a world not designed for you, a world in which you get told there's something wrong with you every day of your life?" These kids typically get few rewards and a great deal of punishment, as if they were always intentionally choosing to become distracted from their homework and forgetting to do their chores. Brenda made an excellent point. It's always important to look not only at people's anger or aggression but also at their environment and whether it encourages or discourages these reactions.

People can have frontal lobe damage without developing full-blown symptoms of ADHD. A stroke or a blow to the head due to a fight or accident could be enough to impair a person's impulse inhibition skills. It's also quite likely that some people are simply born without the qualities necessary for developing good impulse control. However, most people can develop and improve this skill. I'll discuss specific ways to do this in chapter 7.

DIFFICULTIES SHIFTING GEARS

Norman Doidge, in his excellent book *The Brain That Changes Itself* (2007), notes that three specific areas of the brain need to work together to allow people to shift gears—to let go of one concern or task and get on to the next. These are the orbitofrontal cortex (located at the front of the brain), the cingulate gyrus (located above the corpus callosum, which connects the two brain hemispheres), and the caudate nucleus (located deep in the center of the brain). Norman Doidge notes that researchers have discovered that people with obsessive-compulsive disorder have excessive activity in all three of these areas (Doidge 2007). But as with ADHD, I believe many people who don't have full-blown obsessive-compulsive disorder may very well have problems in these areas of the brain that contribute to problems with anger.

What happens when people become angry about something and can't shift gears? Here's an example. I used to counsel a couple: Terry, an accountant in his early forties, and Charlotte, a stay-at-home mom. They had a son named Troy, who was a typical teen. When he was told to take out the garbage, he sometimes did it. But usually he said, "Yeah, I'll do that as soon as I finish…" and then promptly forgot about it. When faced with this normal adolescent behavior, parents usually sigh, get a little annoyed, and say something like "How many times do I have to tell you to take out the garbage, Troy?" End of story—time to get on with life.

Unfortunately, Terry's gearshift often got stuck. He would tell Troy to take out the garbage; Troy would stall, and Terry would take that personally. He'd check back in a few minutes, then in another few minutes. "Have you taken out the garbage yet?" "When are you going to take out the garbage?" Each time he got angrier, until inevitably he burst out with shaming verbal attacks: "Troy, you are a lazy, good-for-nothing, spoiled rotten useless waste of energy." Of course, this verbal abuse only pushed Troy away, and eventually Troy became passive-aggressive against Terry, intentionally putting things off just to bother him.

But the trouble didn't stop there. Terry would keep thinking about how Troy had offended him. He'd bring it up over and over again with Charlotte, who fell into the role of defending Troy. That's what ultimately brought them to counseling. Charlotte was sick of the angry triangle that had developed in their family. She told Terry that if he didn't learn how to let go of his anger at Troy, she would end the marriage. I have to admit that Terry never got really good at deactivating his anger, although he did improve enough to save his marriage. Unfortunately, he never really understood that he had to let go of the bad he saw in Troy in order to notice the good.

The people I see who have gear-shifting problems are often mired in hate. Someone harmed them badly in the past. Perhaps it was a cheating partner, a dishonest business associate, a mean brother or sister, or an abusive parent. The offense is long over. Still, these people keep thinking obsessively about what happened. Worse, every time the memory comes up, these people feel reinjured, as if they are being betrayed in that moment. They just cannot let go of their pain.

TEMPORAL LOBE MALFUNCTION

Some people are born with temporal lobe problems, and others develop these problems due to injury. Because the temporal lobes are located at the sides of the head, they are particularly vulnerable to injury. This brain region includes the amygdala and other parts of the limbic system, so injury to the temporal lobes may result in sudden, nearly uncontrollable bouts of rage.

To give you an idea of how this kind of rage manifests, let's look at the situation of Celeste, a fifty-year-old woman with a history of cocaine and methamphetamine addiction. She had been clean for five years but believed the drug abuse had caused brain damage. She said she never had problems with anger before she started using, but afterward she struggled to contain her rage. What bothered Celeste most was that she sometimes experienced blackouts during rages. She said, "I'll be having a disagreement with my husband, Aaron. We'll be at the table fighting over bills or the kids, and I'll feel myself starting to go nutty. Sometimes I can stop if I get away immediately. But last week I tried to make one last point. Aaron says I stopped in midsentence, stood up, and swore a blue streak. Then I threw dishes at him and tried to strangle him. Aaron said I was so strong he couldn't get me off him. He had to ask our son for help. I don't remember any of this happening." Apparently this rage attack lasted about twenty minutes. Afterward Celeste felt absolutely exhausted, as if she'd run a marathon.

These kinds of scary rage attacks frequently seem to be initiated in the temporal lobes. They resemble epileptic seizures in some ways, as the person who has them loses control and has amnesia about the episode afterward. It's quite possible that during these events the brain's electrical patterns change drastically, with too many circuits firing simultaneously and overloading the person's conscious awareness. Let me add that these rages are not the same as alcohol- or drug-induced blackouts. However, they may sometimes be related, in that the brain damage from substance abuse increases the likelihood of such rages.

Studies have also looked into other abnormal electrical patterns in the brain related to anger and aggression. For example, there appears to be a connection between aggressive criminal behavior and having slower-than-normal brain wave patterns (Ellis 2005). However, the specific causes for these brain wave variations has not been discovered and research on this topic is generally inconclusive.

Summary

Clearly, there are many possible explanations for how and why some people become angry frequently. Some causes cited above, such as frustration, are as much social as individual in origin. Others arise within the brain, such as certain types of brain damage. Note that I've included an appendix in which I describe medications that might be useful for individuals with difficult anger problems. However, my working assumption from this point on is that people with anger problems can learn to become less angry.

Chapter 5

You Can Change Your Brain

This could be the single most important chapter in this book. The neuroscience explained here will assure you that it is indeed possible to transform your angry brain into one that is calmer and less quick to react. It also provides a bridge between chapters 1 through 4, which focused on how the brain, and specifically an angry brain, functions, and chapters 6 through 8, which focus on helping you design your own plan for change.

Neuroplasticity

Let's begin with an overview: Two types of learning must occur in order to make a meaningful change in regard to anger. First, you must develop and maintain new, anger-reducing ways of thinking and behaving. Second, you must quit using old, anger-increasing patterns. Although it would be best for those two changes to take place simultaneously, initially it is probably more efficient to put a great deal of energy into developing new behaviors. The reason is simple enough: it's harder to unlearn old brain patterns than it is to learn new ones. But fortunately, as you'll soon learn, concentrating on learning new behaviors will probably result in reduced reliance on your old habits. In effect, strengthening the set of new behaviors you desire will weaken older behaviors.

Brain changes take place within neurons and in the tiny spaces between them—the synapses. Two important terms used to describe these changes are neuroplasticity and long-term potentiation. *Neuroplasticity* refers to the brain's amazing lifelong ability to change how its neurons interact with each other. *Long-term potentiation* is the process by which these changes take place and are retained. I'll describe this process in some detail, but rest assured that you don't need to remember any specific steps. Instead, just try to get a feel for what's going on inside your brain every time you make a serious effort to alter your behavior.

One word of advice before we jump in: Neuroplasticity doesn't come easy. If you want to transform your angry brain into one that's more peaceful, you'll need to make a strong and continuing commitment to the process.

Use It or Lose It

If your brain had a motto it might be this: "Always strive for maximum efficiency and moderate flexibility." Maximum efficiency is necessary because the brain utilizes a tremendous amount of energy. That little two- to three-pound organ uses about 20 percent of the body's glucose. This gluttonous energy demand is the reason that humans can't simultaneously fly like a bird, run like a gazelle, smell as well as a dog, and see as acutely an eagle. Each of these skills takes a lot of brainpower. You'd need a brain the size of a suitcase to do everything exceptionally well, and you'd probably need to consume tens of thousands of calories. Instead, each species has developed the ability to do a few things well. Thinking, especially abstract thinking, is our particular human specialty.

Moderate flexibility is necessary because we live in a constantly changing world. Summer morphs into winter and we need an entirely different set of skills to survive. Friends become foes, and enemies become allies. Your car hits a patch of ice and you need to shift quickly into survival mode. Cell phones replace land lines. A job ends and a new career begins. A baby is on the way. Your brain needs to anticipate, prepare, and adapt to all these changes, and that calls for flexibility. However, flexibility is a mixed blessing. We also need stability. Too much flexibility feels chaotic, while too little produces rigidity. If you were lost in a forest you would need to use your flexibility to find a way out. But then you would need stability to keep walking that path.

Neuroscientists have studied how the brain provides both efficiency and flexibility. The phrase they use that best summarizes the dynamic is "Use it or lose it." Here's an example of what this phrase is getting at: Imagine that a man named Harry was cutting wood with a chainsaw when he accidentally amputated his left index finger. As it turns out, Harry is a neuroscientist with access to modern imaging machines, and just by coincidence he'd recently completed imaging a map of his brain in action that showed the location of each finger's brain map. (A *brain map* is the area in the brain that activates when a particular part of the body is moved or a task is performed.) That map revealed that the brain region controlling the index finger is located next to the brain regions for the other fingers. After his accident, Harry decided to make a new image of his brain finger maps every few weeks. He soon discovered that the neurons that formerly lit up when he used his index finger were being taken over by his other fingers. In essence, his brain decided that since his index finger was gone, it would put those resources to a new use rather than let them be wasted.

That example of "use it or lose it" is pretty literal. But the same principle applies to many situations in which people are either actively developing or seriously neglecting a skill. If a person is learning to play the piano and keeps at it in a dedicated way, the brain map for the areas linking music and hand-eye coordination will grow. But where will the neurons making up that map come from? Perhaps from an area involved in a related skill, such as gymnastics, that the person no longer practices. Likewise, if a person decides to become more caring and compassionate and actively cultivates those qualities, the neurons needed to improve in those areas will come from a related but relatively underused brain network.

"Use it or lose it" is an incredible concept in regard to the brain. For generations scientists believed that the brain never changed and that each area of the brain served one and only one purpose. They thought that neurons couldn't be repurposed. They also believed that once a function was lost, it was gone forever. Even twenty-five years ago, when I was a social worker at a hospital's brain trauma rehabilitation center, this kind of thinking permeated the atmosphere. But modern brain imaging techniques and experiments have shown that the brain is anything but static and fixed. Instead, the neurons within the brain are constantly forming and reforming neural networks that may consist of hundreds of thousands of cells.

Some neuroscientists refer to the "use it or lose it" concept as "neural Darwinism," meaning that they envision the neural networks within the brain as constantly competing to gain speed, volume, and influence. So when one neural network is weakened through disuse, other neural networks that are highly active and growing will commandeer some of those vulnerable neurons.

In this view of things, it could seem as though there's a war going on inside your head. However, these events can also be interpreted as cooperative. Imagine a neuron named Teresa, from neural network A, having a nice chat with Albert, from neural network B: "Albert, I see you're not being used much right now. You look like you're kind of wasting away over there. We have an opening for you in our network. You'll be busier and you'll get faster, stronger, and more effective by coming to work for us. How about it?" Teresa is recruiting Albert. By the way, the neurons most likely to be recruited are those at the edges of a neural network. Relatively speaking, they are less crucial to the old network. Also, as mentioned in chapter 1, any single neuron may be involved in several neural networks at the same time.

"Use it or lose it" is an essential concept for learning to manage anger and aggression. You must practice, practice, practice your developing skills over an extended period of time in order to build a strong neural network. If you quit practicing your new skills on a daily basis, your neural network will quickly weaken and perhaps wither away altogether.

Neurons That Fire Together Wire Together

"Use it or lose it" describes what you need to do to achieve significant brain change. But exactly what happens within your brain when you make these changes? That's where the famous saying (originally spoken by neuroscientist Carla Shatz) "Neurons that fire together wire together" comes into the picture (Doidge 2007, 63). In this section I'll describe the basics of this process, steering clear of most of the complicated details that scientists are just beginning to comprehend.

Let's start with an example of a very realistic scenario: Imagine that you realize that part of your anger problem stems from having parents who were often critical and seldom praised you, each other, or anybody else. Not surprisingly, you grew up to be an adult who is often critical and seldom gives praise. But now you are a parent yourself, and you want to help your kids feel better about themselves than you feel about yourself. You decide that one important way to do so is to give them praise whenever they've earned it, rather than always finding fault. You begin a daily regimen of giving praise. Every morning you remind yourself to offer your children praise and positive feedback, and then you make sure you actually do so several times a day. Gradually you get better at this particular skill. Eventually you discover, to your joy, that it has become easier to give your children praise. (And, not coincidentally, given the "use it or lose it" rule, you also find it harder to give them criticism.)

Before long, your partner and other family members start to mention how happy they are that you say such nice things to them. Your coworkers tell you that they appreciate the positive feedback you give them. Plus, your friends and family seem to enjoy your presence more than ever. You realize that your new skills around giving praise rather than criticism have become almost automatic and have spread beyond their original target (your kids) to the rest of your world. In this scenario, you've made long-term changes in your brain. The neural connections—the neural networks or maps—look different. This is an example of neuroplasticity in action.

Neural networks form because the mammalian brain is good at associating thoughts and events that happen at nearly the same time. This is the principle of association, mentioned in chapter 4, at work. Humans are capable of putting together long chains of associations. For example, the whole concept of deferred gratification, in which we put off immediate pleasure in order to get a better reward later, is an associative chain. This kind of chain takes years to develop. That's where patient parents come in, as they gradually lengthen the time between a child's stimulus and reward: "Not now, honey. We'll play computer games after supper. That will sure be fun, won't it?"

Not all neural chains make rational sense. The superstitious gambler making ridiculous arm movements because he thinks they'll bring him luck has developed a neural network that might lead to the poorhouse. Another example is a paranoid husband who puts dubious clues together to convince himself his wife is cheating; for example, she came home thirty minutes late and she mentioned that she saw Joe at the mall, therefore she must be having an affair with Joe. He has developed a network that might take lead to divorce, jail, or even murder. A neural network can be debilitating, as with a survivor of childhood sexual abuse who now associates any man's sexual interest in her as terrifying. The label for this type of neural network is "post-traumatic stress disorder." As you can see, you need to be careful about the kinds of neural networks you consciously decide to develop in the area of anger management. You need to think of both what you want to do and what you want to avoid.

Now let's take a closer look at what's going on within the brain to create these long-term changes, or neuroplasticity. It's useful to divide the process into three parts:

- Building a neural network

- Improving the network

- Expanding the network

That list looks nice and tidy. Of course, as you know now, brain processes are extremely complex and involve a great deal of feedback and modulation. So be aware that these three aspects of the development of new neural networks overlap a lot. In actuality, the network is simultaneously building, improving, and expanding.

Building a Neural Network

When you develop a skill set, your brain recruits available neurons to form a network. As they become coordinated, these neurons actually do begin to fire together, meaning that the electrical discharge of all of the neurons in the network takes place virtually simultaneously. The result is a strong discharge that eventually leads to effective muscle movements, hormone release, or any number of other functions.

I like to think of neurons connecting to make a well-functioning network as if they were athletes at relay races in the Summer Olympics.

During a relay race, runners finishing their leg of the race must pass a baton to a teammate who will take over for a leg and then become the next baton passer. Sure, once in a while the handoff is muffed. But usually the talented Olympic athletes make something challenging look easy. It's remarkable how these runners accomplish a difficult feat with such grace.

These athletes are like your brain's neurons in many ways. For one thing, when they first begin practicing with each other, they aren't nearly as good at passing the baton as they later become. Initially they have to move slowly, and they have to practice their handoffs again and again until they get good at it. Brain neurons start communicating with one another slowly as well, only gradually improving their speed of connection. Secondly, there may come an "aha!" moment, a breakthrough when everything falls into place and what had been difficult and unwieldy becomes much easier to accomplish. Suddenly the struggling runners find their rhythm. The baton gets passed in a blur, as if the athletes had been working together all their lives. Neural networks can act in this fashion as well. Part of that process comes about when the neurons in the network develop a coating of myelin; as mentioned in chapter 1, this is a layer of fat that acts as insulation and speeds communication. Thirdly, the runners have to get good at both receiving the baton and passing it off to the next runner, which is similar to a neuron first receiving a signal at a dendrite from its predecessor and then passing that signal along its axon to another neuron. And lastly, the runners gradually become so good at what they do that they don't have to think about it. Individual neurons don't think, of course, but the faster and more automatically they act, the less you have to think consciously about your actions.

The brain, of course, is far more complicated than a relay race. Imagine that you're the runner (a single neuron) about to receive the baton. To improve the analogy, here's what I should add:

- Instead of one racer passing a baton there could be up to ten thousand of them simultaneously handing them off. They are all making contact with you, some of them tapping you on the head, some pressing the batons into your chest, and so on. Amazingly, you are able to grab each and every one of those batons. This is exactly what happens as multitudes of neurons send messages from their axons to the dendrites of the receiving neuron.

- Some of the batons you receive come with a message to speed up, while others tell you to slow down. That's because the brain has two kinds of neurotransmitters that cross the synaptic gap, the tiny gap between neurons where communication must occur chemically, rather than electrically. Some of these neurotransmitters are excitatory, telling the receiving neuron to fire its own electrical charge (as mentioned in chapter 1, the excitatory chemical is typically glutamate). Other neurotransmitters are inhibitory, telling the neuron not to fire (primarily GABA). Whether or not the receiving neuron fires depends on the relative number and strength of the signals from the two sets of competing influences.

- Each baton has a special shape, just like the neural receptors. Neurons are fussy creatures. They won't accept just any old neurotransmitter into any receptor. Instead, the neurotransmitter must fit into a receptor on the receiving neuron just like a key fits into a lock.

I should note that the idea of *building* a neural network may be somewhat inaccurate. These systems aren't created from scratch in adults. However, neural networks probably do change their level of arousal, routing pathways, and many other processes, and these changes indicate the remarkable plasticity of the human brain.

Improving the Network

Let's continue with the analogy of Olympic athletes. Imagine that you're a relay runner and you and your coach are viewing recordings to compare your early and more recent performances. "Wow," says your coach. "Look at how much better you've gotten at holding your arms in, maintaining your pace, and pushing off with every step you take." Essentially, you've improved multiple aspects of your running to get so good at it. That's exactly what happens at the level of neurons and synapses as a neural network improves.

Researchers have discovered at least four ways that the neurons change at the synapse that together help improve the speed and strength of signal transmission. Together, these changes are a significant compo-nent of long-term potentiation because once they occur, they persist indef-initely. And if you want to make lasting changes in how you do things, long-term potentiation must occur. Ultimately, behavior changes such as becoming less critical and giving more praise depend on your brain mak-ing microscopic alterations in its basic neural structure. Here are the four major changes that take place at the synapse in long-term potentiation.

More receptor sites become available. As a neural network forms, neu-rons start firing together. This increases the strength of incoming mes-sages at the receptor sites on the receiving neuron (called the postsynaptic neuron, in contrast to the presynaptic neuron on the sending side of the synaptic gap). The stronger input opens small channels in the neuron into which calcium flows. This in turn makes more receptor sites available—sites that the neuron had been holding in reserve—allowing the receiving neuron to take in more neurotransmitters. If that neurotransmitter is glu-tamate, the neuron is now doubly activated. That's like the coach not just cheering you on but handing you a beverage high in electrolytes as you run by. More receptors means a higher neuronal activity level.

Receptor sites stay open longer. As long-term potentiation develops, postsynaptic receptors, old and new, also begin staying open longer. Again, the result is that more neurotransmitters get into the cell. A neuron with higher levels of neurotransmitters has a greater readiness to fire. However, it is possible for neurotransmitter levels to get too high. Too much gluta-mate, in particular, can kill cells. That's like an athlete training too hard and causing damage to muscles and nerves.

The shape of receptor sites changes to facilitate neurotransmitter uptake. The third major change is that the shape of the area of the neu-ron where receptor sites are located changes. You can imagine receptor sites as numerous places for boats to dock along a narrow pier (called a dendritic spine). The pier (the dendritic spine) sticks out into the water (the synapse). Now think about how awkward it is to unload stuff from arriving boats because the pier is so narrow. Maybe only one person at a time can walk on the pier. But what if you could widen the pier so a couple of people could walk on it at the same time? That's essentially what happens at the dendritic spine. Its shape is flattened, with the effect that it presents less resistance to incoming neurotransmitters. Now instead of one person walking slowly and carefully along a narrow pier, you can visualize several people moving swiftly back and forth.

The transmitting neuron delivers more neurotransmitters. The fourth change is the most amazing one of all because it occurs in the sending (presynaptic) neuron, rather than the receiving (postsynaptic) neuron. It turns out that the receiving neuron sends back some messengers (in the form of chemicals) that tell the sending cell to increase its output of neurotransmitters. That's a little like you telling your coach to work harder. The presynaptic neuron apparently gets the message, because it does indeed increase its output of glutamate or other neurotransmitters.

Each of these changes, multiplied by their occurrence at thousands of receptors, increases the speed and strength of the electrical charge in the receiving neuron. In turn, that makes the receiving neuron much more likely to fire, sending out its own messengers and greatly increasing the potency of the entire neural network.

Expanding the Network

Like many people who grew up with financial hardship, I emerged into adulthood with a tendency to be very careful with money. I tried to spend only when I really needed to. Sometimes I held back too long, frustrating my wife, Pat, because I was actually costing us money by trying to save money. Eventually, I realized I needed to change my habits, so I started to spend a little more. As I practiced this behavior I got better at it until I could honestly say I was much more comfortable doing things like giving money to charities than I had been before.

Then one day a client named Suzanne made a fascinating offhand comment: "I never date men who are stingy with their money because men who are tight with money are also tight with their emotions." Sure, that's a huge generalization, but it caught my attention. Soon thereafter I made a promise to myself that I would become more generous in general. I quickly discovered that it's possible to be generous not only with money, but also with emotions, giving praise, cultivating nonjudgmental thoughts about other people and their opinions, trying out new ideas and behaviors, and more. I developed a daily routine, which I maintained for a year, of beginning each morning with a vow to be generous in at least one way that day and ending each evening by reviewing my day to see whether I had kept my promise. Gradually, being more generous in numerous ways became more automatic, so I didn't have to think long and hard every time an opportunity for generosity arose.

To summarize, an idea caused me to reflect upon my behavior. That allowed me repeatedly to change what I did in situations where it might be possible to be generous. This change of behavior slowly reshaped my neural networks until they became more biased toward generosity. In other words, generosity eventually became my mind's rule, rather than an occasional exception. I believe that this is an example of building, improving, and expanding a particular neural network.

One way neural networks expand is by recruiting existing neurons into the group. Certain areas of the brain, including the hippocampus, also create new neurons (a process known as *neurogenesis*). It's possible that these newly developed neurons could be added to an expanding network, though that remains to be proven.

In addition, individual neurons do something that's pretty remarkable. Their dendrites can grow new branches that spread out. Just like a tree, the dendrite sends out large branches, which develop smaller branches, which in turn develop even smaller branches. In honor of this similarity between trees and neurons, this process is called *arborization*. Arborization allows each dendrite to contact and influence hundreds or even thousands of other neurons. In this way, the neural network becomes not only larger, but also far denser.

How to Change Your Brain

Build a neural network, improve the network, and expand the network—this is the formula for achieving significant and long-lasting brain changes. This is what you need to do to calm your angry brain and become a less angry person. Still, at this point it's all conceptual, so let's look at what you need to do to bring about this type of change in your brain.

Various writers and researchers suggest a number of ways to promote neuroplasticity, or long-term potentiation. For example, it helps to have a lot of energy, so a healthful and sufficient diet and regular aerobic exercise are certainly important. Some authors advocate mindfulness—attending to your present-moment experience—as a way to train your brain. They note that mindfulness training and meditation practice teach you how to concentrate your entire mind upon what's going on both inside and outside your body. Another approach is exposure to novelty, which certainly encourages your brain to expand its networks. Additionally, psychotherapy, in the form of talk therapy, may be very useful for people who need to break out of harmful patterns of thinking and behaving. In his book *The Neuroscience of Psychotherapy* (2002), neuropsychologist Louis Cozolino points out that therapy is a safe place to experiment with making otherwise scary changes. Therapy creates a context where people can experience and respond to a moderate stress level—just enough to provide motivation but not so much as to overwhelm.

Although they advocate many different approaches, almost all experts on this topic absolutely agree that there are two essential components to creating long-term potentiation: focused attention and repetition.

Focused Attention

You cannot create long-term potentiation by "kinda, sorta" wanting it. You cannot create it by "trying" to change. And, truly, as noted by many people in recovery from substance abuse, half measures will get you nowhere. Instead, you must want to change with every fiber of your being. Whatever long-term changes you seek, you must make them a top priority in your life.

Focused attention is purposeful, deliberate, and intentional. It involves making a commitment to achieving a particular state of mind. Furthermore, this goal must be completely yours, not someone else's. You must take total ownership. This is particularly true in the area of anger management. I see this in my practice, where angry clients are often sent to me courtesy of unhappy parents or partners, lawsuit-fearing employers, and even judges and probation officers.

Sure, these clients can make at least temporary changes in their behavior, such as quitting drinking for a while and keeping their mouths shut a little more frequently. And maybe that's enough to keep a job or salvage a relationship. But because they came to counseling to fulfill the wishes or demands of others, all too often their positive changes don't last beyond a few weeks or months. That's when a now former client tells off her boss and gets fired. That's when a partner appears in my office with complaints: "He was so wonderful for a while. I really thought he had changed. But now he's back to yelling and bullying, just like before he went into treatment." These clients did alter some of their actions, but they didn't change their brain. Long-term potentiation didn't occur because these people weren't motivated to do more than the minimum required to satisfy others.

Simply put, you must make a serious long-term commitment to change your brain. It must be a high enough priority that you think about it daily for weeks if not months. My personal belief is that most genuine brain changes take six months to a year or more of sustained attention.

Repetition

Changing your brain takes time and effort. So once you begin to learn specific techniques in chapters 6 through 8, you'll need to practice, practice, practice. But be careful here. It's all too easy to practice doing the wrong things. As mentioned earlier, neuroplasticity can lead to mastering unfortunate behaviors and problematic thinking habits just as easily as good ones. For example, it's important for most angry people to learn to take a time-out. But if you practice, practice, practice taking time-outs until you use them almost immediately over any small conflict, you'll actually be doing more harm than good. A time-out is a specific anger management tool that's appropriate in certain situations. It's just one of many a person needs to master to calm an angry brain.

That brings to mind something I call the substitution principle: It's never enough to set a goal of stopping undesired behavior. You must also have a clear idea about what kinds of positive behavior you intend to develop. Here are twelve examples of positive behaviors to cultivate in place of behaviors you'd like to avoid.

Brain network you want to diminish	Brain network you want to develop
Looking for what's wrong with people	Looking for the good in people
Being quick to criticize and slow to praise	Being quick to praise and slow to criticize
Exaggerating problems; making mountains out of molehills	Keeping problems in perspective
Saying the first thing you think when you're mad	Taking several seconds before you say anything when you're upset
Thinking only about yourself	Practicing empathic listening to better understand others
Taking a stance of distrust and paranoia	Giving people the benefit of the doubt
Keeping your thoughts and feelings to yourself	Regularly sharing your thoughts and feelings
Jumping to negative conclusions	Waiting until you get all the facts before making a decision
Hanging on to old grudges and resentments	Letting go of grudges and practicing forgiveness
Settling conflicts with your fists	Talking through your conflicts
Acting in a controlling manner	Discussing issues from a perspective of equality
Running away from your problems	Facing your problems directly

Those suggestions give you a good idea of directions you want to travel in, but as goals, most of them are incomplete. To make them achievable, you need to add specific behaviors so you'll know when you've accomplished your aim. For example, what exactly does it mean to discuss issues from a perspective of equality? It could mean turning off the television during conversations so you can listen to others respectfully, reminding yourself during a conversation that another's person's point of view is worth considering, or sharing the checkbook and financial planning with your partner. These are just a few of the many possibilities.

Once you have these specific and clear goals in place, you'll know what thoughts and actions you should repeat as often as possible. In short, that's how you ensure that you're utilizing neuroplasticity to improve your life.

One specific form of repetition is worth mentioning: massed practice. *Massed practice* occurs when you do some specific activity or routine frequently, perhaps as often as several times a day. How does this help? Remember that neuroplastic changes in the brain are competitive. The more often you activate a particular network, the stronger it becomes relative to competing networks. So if I've set a goal of speaking softly even when I'm excited about something, then every time I do so instead of shouting I am simultaneously strengthening one network and diminishing the other.

An Example of Neuroplasticity in Action

An excellent example of neuroplasticity in the area of anger management is HEALS, a program created by Steven Stosny. This program is a powerful way to transform resentments against someone who harmed you into compassion for that person. People who make this transformation find themselves freed from the burden of hatred and, simultaneously, are able to embrace their higher-level moral selves. Steven Stosny has kindly given me permission to share the outline of his program here.

Developing Compassion

HEALS is one of an increasing number of programs or interventions based on a model of intrinsic human compassion. *Compassion* refers to the natural human ability to care for others, to suffer their pain with them, to want to help those who are in pain, and to empathically link with others' emotions. The neurological basis for compassion may come from what are now called *mirror neurons*. These neurons are activated both by your own actions and by those same actions of another person. I'll describe mirror neurons in detail in chapter 8.

It's best to think of the human capacity for compassion as a potential, rather than a given. It's likely that there are many genes that help a person become compassionate, not just a single gene. But as is usually the case, just because we are born with certain genes doesn't guarantee that those genes will be activated. (The official term for gene activation is *gene expression*). In all likelihood, genes that further compassion must be encouraged to activate. That's where loving, kind, and caring parents and other adult nurturers enter the scene. They repeatedly teach particular ways to show compassion, such as sharing toys or treats with a friend. More than that, they provide the safe and nurturing environment in which the capacity for compassion can thrive.

It's certainly possible for people to reach adulthood without developing much compassion. These people may have inherent brain deficits or may have suffered specific brain injuries. But brain damage probably isn't the main reason for failing to develop compassion. Rather, the primary cause is growing up with dangerous, abusive, neglectful, non-nurturing adults, which teaches children that they'd better fend for themselves and distrust everyone else. Indeed, some people who grew up in such situations end up being labeled sociopaths because they seem to have virtually no compassion for others. However, even these people, as wounded as they are, can develop at least some compassion if they are taught empathy skills and given plenty of time to practice them, and if they are in a safe environment where these skills are rewarded. In my practice, I've encountered many people who grew up in non-nurturing environments and entered into severely violent and cruel criminal worlds during adolescence and early adulthood. Yet as maturing adults, they consciously chose to discard that way of life. They turned their lives around by developing compassion, a skill they learned by following the advice and copying the behaviors of compassionate friends, loved ones, mentors, sponsors, and others.

Letting Go of Resentment

People who have been abandoned or betrayed by those they trusted often have trouble letting go of their pain. They repeatedly think about what happened. But as mentioned in chapter 4, every time they do so they feel injured again, so their pain never eases. In terms of neural networks, we could say that they are constantly strengthening a specific network that increases their feelings of resentment and decreases compassion. At its extreme, this fosters hatred.

Because resentment persists longer than a time-limited emotion, it's more like a mood. But whereas most moods go away after an hour or two, resentment can last for years as the person obsesses about being injured, fantasizes about how to exact revenge, and tries to gather allies. The result is a lifestyle of self-generated misery.

Enter Steven Stosny and HEALS. The key to his program is helping people reclaim their core values of compassion from the ash heap of resentment. Stosny believes that our strongest emotions center on our deepest values. These core values provide meaning and purpose to our lives. They are personal, but they are also spiritual in the sense they connect us to each other and to the universe. For most people, these core values include appreciating and protecting those we love (or those we loved before the betrayal occurred). Furthermore, these core values are fundamentally incompatible with resentment. The more we celebrate and practice these core values, the less time we'll have for revisiting our grudges. Stosny emphasizes that the core value of self-compassion—sympathy for the hurt and vulnerability causing anger and resentment, with a motivation to heal and improve—is necessary to maintain compassion for others. Failure of self-compassion makes it difficult to recognize the hurt of others, much less care about it. Because the well-being of loved ones is inextricably linked to personal well-being, self-compassion and compassion for loved ones must be simultaneous. One without the other will produce pain and suffering.

The goal is to find a way to build up the neural network associated with these core values so that the network associated with resentment will diminish.

Building New Responses

A conscious transformational process is all well and good, but as I've mentioned, anger and resentment can be triggered almost instantaneously. This can occur at the subconscious level and produce physical and emotional changes before you realize what's happening or are able to intervene. Steven Stosny goes so far as to state that the standard techniques of anger management don't work because anger management requires a conscious effort to handle an unconscious process. Therefore, his goal is to build a conditioned response that automatically and immediately leads people to respond in keeping with their core values even in the face of situations that might trigger resentment. To do so, he helps his clients develop the habit of compassion through massed practice in the form of specific, one- to two-minute exercises to be done twelve times a day for six weeks. I highly recommend his program (available at compassionpower. com), but if you'd like to get a feel for what it involves, you can try the streamlined approach outlined below:

1. Think of a time you felt hurt and angry. Let yourself start feeling aroused, feeling the pain and anger physically and thinking angry thoughts. Then mentally flash the word "HEALS" over the face of the offender. This is the "H" in HEALS. Vividly seeing this word in your mind cuts off the negative reaction and starts you on an inward journey toward your core values.

2. "E" represents *experience*, namely your willingness to experience your own deep hurts within your resentment—hurts that are expressed in phrases such as "I feel unlovable" or "I feel inadequate." The past events that gave rise to these wounds may have been deeply shameful, casting light on how resentments are often a blend of anger, shame, and the fear of rejection.

3. "A" represents *accessing* your core values, particularly self-compassion and compassion for others. The strength of this powerful value is what allows you to let go of resentment and develop more positive feelings toward the offender.

4. "L" represents *loving* yourself by loving others. Stosny suggests that you have to act in a loving manner to be lovable. More specifically, at this stage you connect with the offender's core wound, which is often the same as your own.

5. "S" stands for *solving* the problem by discovering behavioral alternatives to acting on resentments. These alternatives are much easier to generate once you aren't caught in the vise grip of resentment.

Let's do some multiplication. Practicing HEALS twelve times a day times over a period of six weeks generates a total of 504 practice sessions. That can be enough for you to develop an immediate, automatic, and preconscious pathway to compassion. A neural network supporting compassion will be built (actually rebuilt) and improved. The HEALS program also provides a way to expand this neural network: Each day, you're asked to add one new activity that supports your core value of self-compassion and compassion for others. With time, you can point to more and more small acts of caring and compassion that you do on a daily basis. In this way, the neural network expands from extending compassion to one particular person to treating everyone with caring, and your general approach will be shifted away from hostility and toward compassion.

Summary

Build a neural network, improve the network, and expand the network. Are you ready to do that? Are you ready to make a total commitment to the process? Will you take the time and make the effort to identify specific positive behaviors you want to substitute for old angry reactions? Will you stick to the plan for at least several weeks or, better yet, at least six months? If so, you might want to look back at the twelve examples of positive behaviors to cultivate earlier in this chapter. Do any of them provide a sense of direction? If not, think carefully about what changes you most need make in regard to your anger. Identify the negative thoughts and actions you most want to diminish. Then list some positive actions that could replace those behaviors. Aim for new behaviors that you will have many opportunities to engage in every day.

Check out your ideas with people you trust. They might even be able to add a few helpful suggestions. Then begin every day by reminding yourself of your general goal and the specific ways you intend to achieve that goal. Actively look for opportunities to practice, practice, practice your new behavior so you'll keep getting better at it. Every evening before you go to bed, make sure to review your actions that day and praise yourself for the positive behaviors. Begin small, concentrating on making just a few significant changes. As these become habitual, gradually expand your network of related positive behaviors.

Chapter 6

Recognizing Unconscious Anger Activation

Hopefully you recall that in chapter 3 I divided an anger episode into six components: activation, modulation, preparation, action, feedback, and deactivation. In this chapter I'll focus upon the first two phases of this cycle: activation and modulation. Activation occurs when the brain becomes aroused as it encounters a potentially threatening event. Modulation involves how intensely the brain reacts to the perceived threat. Together, these two stages make up the brain's arousal system.

The Brain's Anger Pathways

Let's revisit the brain's primary anger pathway, which I described in chapter 3:

1. The sensory organs gather information about possible threats, and that information is processed in various regions of the brain.

2. The thalamus, located above the hypothalamus, gathers and organizes this information and transmits it to the amygdala.

3. The medial amygdala is aroused by a possibly threatening stimulus.

4. It sends a message to the medial hypothalamus.

5. The message continues to the dorsolateral PAG (periaqueductal gray), in the midbrain.

6. The PAG triggers motor and autonomic nervous system reactions, resulting in a defensive reaction.

This pathway flows like an underground river beneath full consciousness. Sometimes, though, conscious material is added and then the entire pathway looks like this:

1. The sensory organs gather information about possible threats, and that information is processed in various regions of the brain.

2. The thalamus gathers and organizes this information and transmits it to the amygdala.

3. The medial amygdala is aroused by a possibly threatening stimulus.

4. It sends a message to the medial hypothalamus.

5. The message continues to the dorsolateral PAG, in the midbrain.

6. The thalamus, amygdala, and PAG all send information to the frontal cortex and hippocampus. This information is processed and a conscious decision is made about how to respond.

7. If a show of defensive aggression is warranted, the PAG triggers motor and autonomic nervous system reactions, resulting in a defensive reaction.

Here's the problem I'll address in this chapter: The two initial stages of an anger episode, activation and modulation, usually take place very rapidly and below the level of full consciousness. This means we become angry (activation) and have a surge of adrenaline (modulation) before we know what's happening. It's unrealistic to believe that a powerful emotion like anger could ever be a completely conscious phenomenon. However, learning how to bring angry impulses into conscious awareness as quickly as possible is a realistic goal. Helping you do so is the purpose of this chapter.

Activation, Modulation, and the Amygdala

The brain has many jobs, but first and foremost its task is to ensure our survival. Over countless generations the human brain has evolved a quick-acting neural network for that express purpose. The amygdala is the star of this survival network. When this system works well, the amygdala is quietly content under normal circumstances but rapidly warns us about real dangers. Basically, the job of the amygdala is to quickly appraise stimuli to determine whether they are positive or negative. The amygdala allows us to approach that which is good for us and to avoid things that are dangerous.

Unfortunately, many people develop an overly active warning system. You could say that their amygdalas become too good at what they do. As a result, they send out too many warnings. Furthermore, the warnings are too intense; they're out of proportion to the stimulus. This is like having a very powerful but inaccurate radar system that reports every large bird as an enemy fighter jet zooming in to attack.

Sensing Threats

The amygdala sits in the limbic system at a crossroads between the brain stem and the cortex. This central location makes it the perfect place for an early warning system. It can perform the critical function of connecting more primitive automatic faculties, such as breathing, muscle movement, and other autonomic (involuntary) nervous system reactions, with higher-level thought processes. In addition, information from all of the sense organs arrives at the amygdala quickly, allowing it to begin assessing potentially dangerous situations right away.

The amygdala reacts to virtually all stimuli and assigns emotional meaning to them. To illustrate how this works, I'll discuss how the amygdala responds to possibly threatening facial messages. This is a good place to start, because people's expressions convey their emotions, and the amygdala is particularly adept at gathering information from people's faces. It automatically records and reacts to even extremely subtle facial cues. The first thing the amygdala does in response to a possibly unfriendly facial expression is fast-track a signal to the rest of the brain as if it were shouting, "*Pay attention!* Something important is going on! More information to follow." This puts the brain and body into a state of alertness.

The second task of the amygdala is to decide whether the incoming facial message is positive or negative. This is akin to asking incoming strangers whether they are friend or foe. Note that we each have two amygdalas, one in each half of the brain. The amygdala on the left side of the brain probably processes mostly positive signals, whereas the one on the right is probably more attuned to negative stimuli. Because the amygdala is nonverbal and preconscious, the warnings it sends come in the form of "gut feelings" that a situation is bad. The phrase "Trust your gut" reflects our instinctive belief that such signals are accurate and should be acted upon. But gut messages tend to be vague, generalized, difficult to interpret, and quite possibly inaccurate. Trusting your gut may be exactly the wrong thing to do in many situations, especially if you have impulsive anger issues.

What triggers the amygdala's alarm response? The twofold answer to this question is critical in understanding how people often develop anger problems. First, the amygdala reacts to genetically programmed natural threats: loud noises, anything moving quickly toward you, troubling facial expressions, unfamiliar people, large animals, snakes, and so on. You have no control over these reactions. They just happen. But in humans, these automatic reactions are just a small subset of stimuli we react to. And since we all respond to them in similar fashion, they don't help explain why some individuals become excessively angry.

Enter associative learning. As discussed, the principle here is that any two things that happen to you at essentially the same time will be linked together in your brain. For instance, if a bully wearing a bright red shirt beat you up when you were a kid, you might link bright red shirts with danger. In all likelihood, that will be an unconscious link. You will have long forgotten that ugly event—on a conscious level. Your amygdala, however, hasn't forgotten. It specializes in remembering emotionally significant occurrences. It not only remembers the bully; it has also merged "bright red shirt" with "danger." As a result, decades later you feel vaguely uneasy every time someone wears bright red clothing.

Gauging the Response

Thus far I've been discussing the activation process. But the amygdala also has a significant place in the second phase of an anger cycle: modulation. When it senses a threat, the amygdala orders the release of energizing substances, including the stress hormones epinephrine, norepinephrine, and cortisol. The quantities released depend upon the number of neurons firing at any time and the quantities of neurotransmitters being released. This speaks to the question of just how excited the brain should get about an incoming signal. When out of control, the amygdala tends to say, "This is big—*really, really big*," about everything. That's like believing every problem is a 10 on a scale from 0 to 10.

Of course, as you're now well aware, no part of the brain ever acts alone. This is equally true in regard to how the brain processes emotionally important information. Like the amygdala, the anterior cingulate and orbitofrontal cortex are also highly attuned to facial messages. Most importantly, the brain attempts to balance the amygdala's tendency to sound the alarm with other systems that can switch the alarm off. This deactivation primarily involves the orbitofrontal cortex and the hippocampus.

The Fear-Anger Connection

I see many clients who have high levels of both anger and anxiety. I think this happens because anger and fear both pass through the amygdala, quite possibly reinforcing each other. I suggest that both anger and fear are likely to become activated when people perceive themselves to be in peril. This triggers the well-known fight-or-flight response. Notice, though, that the phrase "fight or flight" implies that people experience just one emotion at a time. I believe that in real life emotions become blended and integrated, especially when they are closely connected, as anger and fear are.

Imagine a squadron of soldiers who suddenly find themselves nearly surrounded by the enemy. I suppose some soldiers might feel only anger and stand their ground to their death, and others might feel only fear, drop their guns, and take off running. But I'd bet that most of them would feel both fear and anger. In response, they might drop back as quickly as they could while still firing their guns. And later, when they recounted their experience, they would probably indicate that they felt both terror and rage, perhaps at the same time or alternating so quickly they seemed simultaneous at the conscious level.

In my practice, new clients generally say they have an anger problem, and this is true. But when they tell me about the situations that trigger their anger, they often look both angry and anxious. A man isn't just furious with his wife for coming home late; he's also afraid she'll never come back. A woman isn't just scared she'll lose her house, she's also enraged at the bankers, who don't seem to care about her family's need for shelter.

To return to a previous example, maybe when you were attacked by that bully in the bright red shirt, you didn't just become scared. Chances are, you also became angry, maybe even enraged. As a result, you associate bright red clothing with anger as well as fear. This isn't an entirely hypothetical example. I once was asked to intervene with a troubled and upset man in the mental health unit of a local hospital. As we were calming him down, the hospital minister showed up wearing a bright red vest. The patient immediately dissociated and attacked. Later he said that he hated the color red, but he couldn't say why. If only his amygdala could speak, we might have discovered why "red" and "anger" were linked in his mind.

I often counsel people who not only become angry too often but also become dangerously aggressive on those occasions. Something that might only annoy others enrages them. This is a modulation problem. They react far too intensely to ordinary insults. It's as if they had encountered a life-threatening situation. Yet when I ask what made them so violently angry, they often can't identify a specific trigger. It usually takes some serious thinking and talking for them to figure it out. I believe their excessive reactions mirror mostly unconscious perceptions of a serious threat. Their alarm system then starts blasting, and they react to a relatively minor threat with rage.

Defensive Anger Triggers

Alarm systems respond to perceived threats. For an elk, threats tend to be very specific and straightforward; for instance, smelling or seeing wolves. But for humans (because of our remarkable powers of associative learning), many kinds of threats can trigger the alarm system. The concept of defensive anger applies to reactions to all sorts of possible threats, most of which aren't physical. Let's take a look at four kinds of nonphysical threats that could trigger a rage response: threats to the sense of social acceptability, the threat of abandonment, the threat of powerlessness, and violations of deeply held values.

One important note about the following discussion: I don't mean to imply that only people who rage are subject to these excessive emotional reactions. They simply represent the extreme. Where most people might react a little too strongly, these individuals completely lose control.

Shame and Threats to the Sense of Social Acceptability

One deep and mostly unconscious fear that most people harbor is the fear of social rejection. One theory about why this is the case is that for hundreds or thousands of generations, anyone cast out of their group had virtually no hope of survival. As a result, the human brain developed the social emotions (shame, guilt, embarrassment, and pride) to protect us against social rejection. When I feel a moment of shame, I know that I've violated my group's rules, norms, and expectations. This allows me to quickly think about what I need to do to get back in the good graces of my community. There is, however, the possibility that I've done something so awful that my group won't let me back in.

The fight and flight reactions can definitely be interwoven in this context. People who are terrified of losing their place in their society may become defensively irate. I call this kind of angry counterattack shame-based rage.

I frequently work with people whose anger problems are closely connected with feelings of shame. They become angry when anyone says or does something that threatens their good name. For example, Victor became violently aroused when he thought his employer was putting him down. He immediately felt tremendous shame and a deep sense that he wasn't good enough. Victor was certain that his boss was rejecting him and reacted to this perceived shaming attack by counterattacking vigorously. He tried to out-shame the shamer by belittling his employer so he would feel even worse than Victor did. This turned into a classic case of creating your own reality: Victor became so belligerent that he was fired and escorted out by a security guard.

As is often the case, Victor's vulnerability to shame was mostly unconscious. All he knew was that sometimes he reacted furiously to perceived criticisms without even knowing why they upset him.

The Threat of Abandonment

What threat can be more deeply seated than the specter of abandonment? In infancy, we depend upon our caregivers to feed, shelter, and protect us. There is a tremendous amount of research on the differences in how children develop when these needs are consistently met versus when caregivers are inconsistent, abusive, negligent, or unavailable. I'll describe these differences in more detail in chapter 8, on empathy. For now, I'll simply distinguish between (a) children who, because of consistent nurturing, develop a secure base from which to engage the world and (b) insecure children. Many insecure children become insecure adults. And many insecure adults harbor tremendous anger toward the world for its failure to help them feel safe.

Again, this anger usually operates at a mostly subconscious level. It tends to arise when insecure people sense an immediate threat of abandonment. For instance, many people who are subject to strong and irrational jealousy become simultaneously scared and angry whenever their partner moves away from them. Even a partner's trip to the grocery store may feel like an abandonment.

The Threat of Powerlessness

Want to get an infant really mad at you? Just hold his or her limbs to prevent movement for a couple minutes. You'll soon discover just how loudly that child can protest! From birth, humans want to be in charge of their own bodies. That desire for personal control is a major component of the "terrible two" stage, in which the word "no" means "I want to be in charge of what I do. That's how I discover who I am." With time, children become adolescents, determined (sometimes defiantly so) to make their own decisions. Still later comes adulthood, with its emphasis on personal autonomy and, eventually, often feisty determination to stay in control of our choices as we get old. Throughout all of these stages we experience the joy of being in control of our lives—and the threat of loss of that control.

One place I often see this threat play out is among participants in domestic violence prevention programs. Most of these people are on probation and must report regularly to their probation officers. And almost unanimously, they hate how much control the probation officer has over them. Of course, how the probation officer treats them makes a difference. These people typically feel less resentful of probation officers who treat them with respect. But even the best probation officers are resented because they have the power to send people back to jail at any time for just about any reason.

Again, this is largely an unconscious process. These people are not going around complaining about their lack of autonomy. But try giving them a homework assignment, and you'll immediately run into resistance. It's not that they can't do the homework or that they think it's useless; on the contrary, most of them really want to learn anger management skills and quit being violent. Nevertheless, they automatically resist authority. As one man told me, "Ron, I've been in prison most of my adult life. Now that I'm out, I hate it when anybody tells me what to do." It's not about good or bad authority. Any authority is a threat to their sense of being in control of their lives.

Violations of Deeply Held Values

Values are visceral. By that I mean that the values we hold most dear have tremendous emotional power. They reside in our hearts as well as our minds, and in our guts as well as our thoughts. Even if we aren't consciously aware of it, we feel our values at the core of our being. For instance, you may have learned on your father's knee that it's your sacred duty to protect other family members from attack. Thirty years later, it doesn't make any difference whether your siblings are in the right. You'll watch their backs even if you get in trouble for doing so.

As another example, maybe one of your strongest values is "Never quit a relationship." In that case, you'd feel sick and guilty if you seriously considered leaving your marriage, even if your spouse was financially unreliable, had drug problems, or was unfaithful. Or you could be like the actor Charlton Heston, who, as president of the National Rifle Association, swore that the only way he'd give up his gun would be when they pried it from his cold, dead hand.

The emotional power that accompanies our most deeply held values goes far beyond whatever conscious reasons we come up with to justify them. Values represent our core assumptions about how everyone should behave. They exist at our unconscious emotional center and therefore are defended by our amygdala-centered alarm systems.

The Unconsciously Controlled Brain

As mentioned, the amygdala's sensitivity to threat is usually balanced by parts of the prefrontal cortex and the hippocampus, with its ability to sense safety. When all goes as it should, the amygdala activates the sympathetic nervous system, with its stimulating functions, when it senses trouble. If it turns out that there isn't a real threat, the prefrontal cortex and the hippocampus shut down the sympathetic nervous system by activating the parasympathetic nervous system, with its calming functions. These two branches of the nervous systems cannot be activated simultaneously. When the parasympathetic nervous system is activated, you relax. However, you might recall that the amygdala sends more neural fibers, or axons, into the prefrontal cortex than the prefrontal cortex sends to the amygdala. As a result, the amygdala holds the trump card. It is powerful enough to overwhelm the prefrontal cortex.

You can probably think of a time when you were simply overwhelmed with emotion. You may have been terrified, furious, incredibly sad, or even so happy you couldn't stop laughing. No matter what emotion or combination of emotions you were experiencing, there was a common denominator: You couldn't think or problem solve very well. Instead, you were a captive of your emotions. Metaphorically, it might be said that the unconscious processes centered around your amygdala had emotionally hijacked your brain.

Unconscious emotional control can be crude, or it can be subtle. Perhaps you go through life with a strong sense that something bad is going to happen sometime soon. It's just a gut feeling, not based on any real evidence. Nevertheless, that sense of imminent doom feels absolutely correct. Worse, it doesn't go away no matter how often you tell yourself that everything is okay. Another possibility is that you can't shake the sense that people are out to hurt you, cheat you, betray you, or abandon you. Maybe you tell yourself not to be so paranoid. But words are only words and thoughts only thoughts. Deep down you *know* that the world is unsafe and that nobody, not even your best friend or your partner, is on your side. And here's a third possibility: You might carry around a sense of anger at the world, an unreasonable readiness to attack verbally and even physically. Again, even though you can't identify any reason for this feeling, you cannot let go of the anger or the accompanying urges to attack.

Unconscious emotional control occurs when your mostly unconscious emotional system overwhelms your mostly conscious ability to regulate your emotions. When that happens, your emotions become activated too quickly and often without cause. They go on too long, with too much intensity.

Combating Unconscious Control of Emotions

As mentioned at the beginning of this chapter, it's unrealistic to believe that a powerful emotion like anger could ever be a completely conscious phenomenon. However, I also suggested that learning how to bring angry impulses into conscious awareness as quickly as possible is a realistic goal. In the remainder of this chapter, I'll teach you a variety of techniques that will help you do this. The first set of techniques will help you identify anger episodes more quickly. The second set will help create an alliance between the conscious and unconscious aspects of your brain, which will help decrease your degree of unconscious control during emotional episodes.

Learning to Identify Anger Episodes Quickly

The first key to gaining better control over unconscious emotional processes is to identify these events as soon as possible, before damage is done. Two good methods for doing so are developing more bodily awareness and taking a time-out.

INCREASING BODILY AWARENESS

Do you know where in your body you first begin to feel your anger? Is it in your chest? Your jaw? Your hands? Do you begin pacing? Does your voice get louder? Does your head start pounding? Over the years, I've been amazed that so many of the angry people I've counseled can't answer this question.

It's highly worthwhile to tune in to physical sensations and other bodily cues. They're like messengers from your unconscious. When you train yourself to develop more bodily awareness, you'll be able to recognize that you're becoming angry, and you can make conscious decisions sooner than if you wait until your conscious mind knows it's angry. This is critically important, because the longer an anger episode goes unchallenged, the stronger it becomes. So attend to the earliest bodily signs of your anger. As you do so, you'll gradually be able to notice even earlier signs, giving you even more control and therefore more choices.

TAKING A TIME-OUT

Taking a good time-out is the single most effective thing you can do when you can't catch an anger episode early enough to short-circuit it and calm down. Time-outs are your best bet in situations where you have to get away before you say or do something you'll regret. A good time-out consists of four steps:

1. **Recognize.** In the previous section, I recommended that you become aware of the early physiological signs that serve as clues that you're getting angry. It's equally important to attend to the last few signs—what you experience physiologically just before you lose control of your anger and strike out verbally or physically. What do you feel, think, say, and do right before you

explode? For instance, you might feel sick, think someone is out to destroy you, start swearing a blue streak, and walk toward the person you're mad at. Use these signs to tell yourself, "I've got to get out of here now!"

2. **Retreat.** Plan several options for time-outs so you'll have ideas for what to do when it's time to retreat. Can you leave the kids? Do you have warm clothing if you need to take a walk around the block? If it's safe for you to drive, do you have access to a vehicle? Maybe all you can do is go to another room where you can close the door and be alone for five minutes. The goal is to get out as fast as you can before you cause trouble—without causing trouble in the process.

3. **Relax.** Go to a safe place, take a walk, listen to calming music, or do something that you find relaxing. Don't go to a tavern, get into an argument with somebody else, drive at unsafe speeds, or engage in other activities that may stimulate you or maintain your anger. Let the anger drain from your body, then wait a bit longer to ensure that you're also calming down at unconscious levels.

4. **Return.** Once you're truly calm, go back to deal with the situation you took a time-out from. If someone else was involved, be willing to sit down and talk rationally with that person—if he or she is willing and able to do so.

Creating an Alliance between the Conscious and Unconscious

The second general approach to combating unconscious control of emotional episodes is to create a good working alliance between the conscious and unconscious aspects of your brain. As you now know, the neurological alarm system that triggers many anger episodes operates primarily outside of conscious awareness. If you want to change how this alarm system functions, you need to find ways of intervening that speak to your unconscious processes. To do so, you'll need to focus on methods that don't rely on conscious processes. Still, you do need to think about these methods, choose the ones most likely to work for you, and commit to using them when necessary.

Fortunately, there are good techniques for influencing unconscious pathways. The ones I'll describe here will help you shift energy from your sympathetic nervous system, which has a stimulating function, to your parasympathetic nervous system, which has a calming function. Most of these techniques are typically thought of as relaxation exercises. They take advantage of the fact that your brain and spinal cord are basically parts of one interconnected system. While it's true that the brain instructs the autonomic nervous system to activate or deactivate, the reverse is also true. If you can affect the autonomic nervous system, and especially if you can switch on the parasympathetic nervous system, that will have reverberations throughout your nervous system. Most critically, it can turn off or at least turn down your amygdala-centered warning system.

DEEP BREATHING

Probably the single easiest and quickest way to activate the parasympathetic nervous system is to take several deep breaths. In fact, I've found this technique so useful that I generally begin each session of my anger management and violence prevention groups with the following deep breathing exercise:

1. Inhale, taking a deep belly breath, in which you can see your abdomen rise as you allow the incoming air deep into your lungs by lowering your diaphragm. As you inhale, count evenly to four. ("One-two-three-four.")

2. Pause for a single count. ("One.")

3. Slowly exhale, again counting evenly to four. ("One-two-three-four.") Note that exhaling fully and slowly is just as important as inhaling.

4. As you finish exhaling, say "twelve" to yourself.

5. Repeat but end with "eleven," then "ten," and so on, counting down to one.

When you first begin to practice this exercise, you'll probably find it helpful to close your eyes so you can focus on your breathing. But once you've practiced this technique often enough that it's almost automatic, you can use it in situations in which you must keep your eyes open, such as when you're driving.

Here are a few variations on the basic technique that you might want to try:

- You may want to inhale through your nose and exhale through your mouth and visualize blowing away your anger, anxiety, and stress.

- You can substitute a phrase such as "relax" as you inhale or exhale. For example, "One-two-relax-four."

- Some people prefer counting upward from one to twelve rather than the opposite.

With time, you may be able gradually to cut down the number of breaths needed to achieve a state of relaxation, perhaps to as little as just a few deep breaths.

Deep breathing seems like an incredibly simple thing to do. It is. Nevertheless, you still need to practice, practice, practice. The more often you go through the steps, the better you'll get at it, and the more automatic the technique will become. Also, don't wait until you're totally stressed-out to practice deep breathing. Deep breathing is most effective when you use it regularly. It's even better at helping you not get anxious than it is at helping you return to a relaxed state after you've gotten angry or anxious.

PROGRESSIVE MUSCLE RELAXATION

Breathing deeply is a simple, straightforward way to stay calm or to quiet yourself when you've begun to get angry, and you can practice it in any situation. But an even more effective approach is to combine deep breathing with full body relaxation, as in progressive muscle relaxation. This approach is especially useful if you unconsciously carry a lot of tension in your muscles.

In addition to relaxing your muscles, progressive muscle relaxation often reduces pulse rate, blood pressure, and respiration rate. All of these changes lessen your susceptibility to anger, since angry people tense their muscles and have elevated heart and breath rates. In essence, this technique involves first tightening major muscle groups, then releasing them. This heightens the sensation of relaxation and also helps you develop more awareness of when your muscles are tense.

Before you begin, spend a few minutes experimenting with the difference between tense and relaxed states. Tighten your fists, really clenching them tightly for about five seconds. Notice the sensations you feel. Then relax your hands for about twenty seconds and pay attention to the tremendous difference between the tensed and relaxed states. Repeat this a few times, then try tensing up a few other body areas, such as your jaw, stomach, or legs, one area at a time.

Now that you've learned a bit about how your body experiences tension and relaxation, you're ready to practice progressive muscle relaxation. Start relaxing either from the tip of your toes upward or from the top of your head downward, focusing on muscle groups one at a time:

- Feet and toes

- Calves and lower legs

- Thighs and upper legs

- Hips and pelvis

- Stomach muscles

- Chest

- Back

- Shoulders

- Neck

- Jaw

- Face (especially the little muscles around your eyes and temples)

- Forehead, top of the head, and back of the head

For each group, first tense the muscles for about five seconds, then relax for about fifteen seconds. Breathe deeply and slowly throughout the entire process.

Don't try to rush through the process! Take as long as you like, but make sure you practice for at least fifteen to twenty minutes so you can really feel your body relaxing. This exercise is so effective that you might fall asleep when you first begin practicing it. That usually happens because it feels so peaceful to be genuinely relaxed. It's fine to enjoy this from time to time, especially if you're sleep deprived. However, you should try to stay awake as you do the exercise. Progressive muscle relaxation is something you'll want to use at any time of the day.

Practice progressive muscle relaxation twice a day for two to three weeks and then daily for six months. After that, you should be able to automatically relax your muscles without going through the various muscle groups or even having to think about it. You might find it most effective to work with an audio recording. There are many versions available, or you can record your own or ask someone with a soothing voice to record it for you. If you make your own recording, you can find detailed scripts online or in many books on relaxation and stress reduction.

If your brain insists on thinking worrisome or distracting thoughts, like "I'm too busy to do this," "This isn't working," "I'm still too mad to calm down," or "What should I make for dinner tonight?" just imagine tying each thought to a balloon and letting it drift away. Don't engage these thoughts by fighting with them; rather, simply let them depart.

After you've practiced the technique a few times, you can forgo the tensing phase if you like. Another variation is to add a few calming thoughts, such as "This feels wonderful," "I have plenty of time," or "I feel safe and calm." Likewise, you might want to add visual, auditory, or tactile images to enhance your experience of relaxation. Perhaps you have a favorite memory of a time when you felt completely at peace with the world. These kinds of memories come with wonderful visual images, sounds, or sensations. For instance, you might recall a time when you were sitting on an ocean beach feeling the warmth of the sun, listening to the surf, and watching pelicans flying silently over the waves. Or perhaps you recall a time when you were rocking in your favorite chair, eyes shut, glad to be alive, and happy with the universe. When you incorporate images like these, you combine conscious with unconscious processes in a way that changes how you interact with the world. And in the process, you are also maximizing positive brain plasticity.

BRAINWAVE BIOFEEDBACK

Brainwave biofeedback refers to techniques that have been developed to help people change the electrical wave patterns in their brain. The best-known brainwave biofeedback program is neurofeedback, which makes use of an electroencephalogram (EEG) machine to instantly monitor and record the rate at which your brain's neurons are firing. Because the electrical signals of any one neuron are far too tiny to be measured in this way, the EEG actually measures the combined firing of tens of thousands of neurons. These patterns of electrical activity in the brain are grouped into various categories based on rate, or frequency, and these are known as brain waves. Four types of waves are typically studied in neurofeedback, and each is associated with particular physical and emotional states:

- **Delta waves:** up to 4 hertz (cycles per second); associated with deep sleep

- **Theta waves:** 4 to 7 hertz; associated with drowsiness and also linked to conscious attempts to inhibit or repress a response (such as aggression)

- **Alpha waves:** 8 to 13 hertz; associated with a relaxed state, as well as inhibition of actions

- **Beta waves:** 13 to 30 hertz; associated with excited, active, busy, or anxious thinking

In neurofeedback, a licensed professional uses the equipment to assess the subject's brain wave patterns and then provides a training program to promote more activity in targeted brain wave frequencies. If you are easily aroused, quickly alarmed, and controlled by the alarm functions of the amygdala, you may benefit greatly from neurofeedback to help your brain spend more time in the alpha state and less in the beta. Achieving this goal would help you to feel more relaxed and less agitated, anxious, angry, and aroused.

It used to be quite a challenge to train people to produce alpha waves. Fortunately, advances in technology have made it easier to train the brain to create more alpha waves. There are many fun, gamelike programs that give you immediate feedback and reward you visually and with sound effects every time you succeed. Nevertheless, you'll probably need twenty or more sessions to achieve long-lasting mastery. However, the time and effort will be well worth it if it helps you become less chronically agitated.

Neurofeedback can help you produce lasting changes in your brain. Beyond mechanically changing the rate at which your neurons are firing, you are also teaching your brain to relate to the world differently and see it as less dangerous. Consequently, your interior alarm system will be activated less often and be less likely to be triggered by nonthreatening situations. And when your amygdala's alarm system does go off, you won't be agitated for as long.

MINDFULNESS MEDITATION

For many decades, Westerners tended to look upon meditative practices with skepticism, at best. I believe that was mostly because the main practices of meditation seem very passive. After all, what good could possibly come from sitting with your eyes closed and chanting a single phrase over and over? Often, attitudes toward meditation were also tinged with doubt or suspicion as people associated it with foreign religions or cults. Yet "meditation" simply means engaging in contemplation or reflection, and "mindfulness meditation" means turning this sort of attention to the present moment and experiencing it without judgment or the need to change what exists. Meditation is perfectly compatible with any religion and akin to the contemplative practices common to most religions.

Also, I think many Westerners mistakenly believe that feeling relaxed means being sleepy or inattentive. However, meditation is actually a state of heightened alertness, even though meditators often report feelings of calmness during a session.

Over time, attitudes toward meditation have changed as people discovered the benefits of meditative practices. One major benefit is helping people in our goal-oriented culture achieve a more balanced state of mind—one that is both relaxed and alert at the same time. As to other benefits, there's a huge body of research indicating that mindfulness meditation is extremely effective for countering the effects of stress, and as you'll recall, stress can be a factor in creating an angry brain.

Now researchers are beginning to illuminate the brain mechanics of meditation. The middle frontal area of the cortex, including the anterior cingulate, becomes highly activated during meditation. The middle frontal cortex is important for emotional balance, cognitive flexibility, development of empathy, and regulation of fear. Furthermore—and this is critical—among experienced meditators the amygdala is far less active than in most people (Brefczynski-Lewis et al. 2007). So if you possess a hyperactive alarm system, meditation could be the key to rewiring that system at a very deep level.

I highly recommend that you give mindfulness meditation a try to see whether you find it helpful. There are numerous practices, and you're sure to find some that are appealing and that you can work into your day. To whet your appetite, I'll outline a couple of practices you might start with, including the first one I ever tried. I call it the Raisin d'Etre (Raisin to Be) Experiment (Kabat-Zinn 1990).

1. Take a single raisin. Examine it closely, noting its color, shape, size, and texture.

2. Place the raisin on the tip of your tongue. Notice its weight on your tongue. Attend to how it feels. Note any taste. Remember not to judge. It's not a good-tasting raisin or a bad-tasting one. It's simply a raisin.

3. Sit quietly and let the raisin moisten and soften in your mouth. Notice how it changes. If you find that you've become distracted, gently bring your attention back to the raisin.

4. Take a tiny bite out of the raisin. What do you taste and feel? If you start getting a little impatient or increasingly distracted, don't judge yourself. It's always difficult to maintain attention. The practice lies in returning your attention to the raisin again and again.

5. Go ahead and s-l-o-w-l-y chew the raisin. Try to concentrate on your experience without working at it. This isn't a job; it's an opportunity.

6. Swallow the raisin, but keep attending to the experience. Your mouth may have a lingering relationship with the raisin. Just experience it, whatever it may be.

This is definitely a different way of relating to food! You may wonder what it has to do with anger. Do you remember that most of the more recently evolved brain structures, especially in the cortex, consist of six vertical layers? Direct experience enters at the lower layers, whereas interpretations of your experience come down from the top layers. So meditation practices in which you tune in to your present-moment experience nonjudgmentally help you experience life from the "bottom up" rather than the "top down." When you really taste that raisin, it's a bottom-up sensation; but when you start thinking about it, it becomes top-down.

With that in mind, here's a meditation experiment that will help you develop a different relationship with your anger:

1. Think about something that tends to trigger your anger episodes. It should be strong enough to activate your alarm system but not so strong you could lose control. As you think about it, allow yourself to feel your emotions and physical reaction. Let your brain and body become anxious and angry. Even in the realm of visualization, an overactive amygdala perceives danger. In response, your muscles are probably tight and your mind is probably tense.

2. Simply watch all of this happening—just observe, without getting caught up in the emotion. It's almost like being at a distance from your own anger. As a result, you're less likely to feel an urge toward action. Instead, focus on the thoughts and feelings created by your brain's amygdala-centered alarm and arousal system.

3. Notice how the wave of anger begins to subside after a few minutes. You don't need to do anything to make the anger go away. You've remained still, and it's departing on its own. You feel safe and calm.

This practice reveals how quiet, focused attention to your own inner processes can help you deal with strong emotions. You can feel them, but you don't have to act on them. And, amazingly, angry feelings will diminish on their own if you let them. After you've done this practice a few times using imagined anger-inducing situations, try it out in real life. See whether you can observe your experience and gain a little distance from your emotions. This may enable you to let the episode fade away, rather than getting involved in an angry reaction.

Think of anger as if it were a forest fire. What puts out a fire? Water, of course—if you have enough of it. But now you've learned another way: Just don't feed the fire. A fire without fuel will go out on its own. That's the secret of mindfulness meditation.

Many teachers of mindfulness meditation recommend that people practice compassion toward themselves. In regard to anger specifically, they believe that you suffer greatly when you get angry. The solution is to first put out the fire in your heart by not feeding the flames. But once you are calm, it's important to attend to whatever caused you to hurt so much. Approach your suffering self as if it were a terrified child lashing out blindly at the world. Comfort, caress, and nurture that child. Hold that angry child until the anger goes away, then teach your wounded self how to smile.

Mindfulness is a skill. Like all skills, it benefits from the brain's ongoing plasticity. The more you practice mindfulness the better you'll get at it.

Summary

Deep breathing, progressive muscle relaxation, neurofeedback, mindfulness meditation—these are four ways to lessen the unconscious control of the amygdala-centered alarm system. Together with increasing your bodily awareness, these strategies can help you learn to notice when an anger episode begins (activation) and how it ramps up (modulation). So as you master these techniques (through practice, practice, practice!) and learn to take a time-out when you need it, you'll help ensure that you handle the first two phases of an anger episode well. Now we can begin to consider the next two phases of an anger episode: preparation and action. Because the techniques you learned in this chapter can help you relax and slow down, they'll buy you some time to consider and choose a response, rather than reacting in habitual ways. Still, there's a lot that can go wrong in the preparation and action stages. To that end, the next chapter will look at how and why the angry brain makes poor choices and then offer some strategies to help you handle these stages of an anger episode well.

Chapter 7

Avoiding Conscious Bad Choices

Why do people make such bad choices when they're angry? In this chapter, I'll endeavor to answer that question. But equally importantly, I'll give you several techniques that can help you make better, less damaging decisions, even when you're extremely upset, allowing you to do a better job of navigating the middle stages of an anger episode: preparation and action.

Decisions, Decisions

For the purposes of this chapter (and this book), I'll define "good choices" as those that are fully conscious, driven by the facts, and unbiased. Four key concepts underlie everything you'll learn in this chapter:

1. It is seldom easy to make good choices.

2. It is much harder to make good choices when you're angry.

3. The angrier you are, the more difficult it will be to make good decisions.

4. Habitually angry people habitually make poor choices because of cognitive distortions that warp their view of reality.

The previous chapter primarily discussed unconscious brain processes. That's because your initial appraisal of any emotionally significant event is primarily unconscious. Unfortunately, the unconscious alarm system can become overactive and inaccurate. But that doesn't mean all anger problems are caused by unconscious processes. On the contrary, angry people tend to be quite adept at making fully conscious bad decisions that lead to unnecessary trouble.

To understand why and how that happens, we must venture into different brain territory. All conscious thinking processes occur in the cerebral cortex, the gray matter that covers the surface of the brain—primarily in the frontal lobe and especially the prefrontal lobe.

The Prefrontal Cortex

The prefrontal cortex is subdivided into several regions. Many of these areas are important when it comes to handling anger well, as mentioned in chapter 3. For instance, the orbitofrontal cortex, located just behind your eyes, helps you understand the rules of your culture, make moral decisions, and apply both in the context of daily living. Meanwhile, the dorsolateral prefrontal cortex, located toward the top and side of the prefrontal cortex, is essential for executive function—the ability to plan and execute a course of action. In addition, the ventrolateral prefrontal cortex, found below the eye region, helps inhibit behavior, which is certainly a critical aspect of anger management. More generally, the middle parts of the prefrontal cortex are involved in the conscious experience of emotions, monitoring one's emotions, and inhibiting excessive emotional reactions and emotion-driven behaviors. The prefrontal cortex helps you be less irritable, have a longer fuse on your temper, feel less unwarranted hostility, and be less likely to commit impulsive acts.

One of the main tasks of the neurons in the prefrontal cortex is aiding in envisioning a sequence of actions taking place in time. Working memory, a type of memory that allows us to focus upon a task, allows the brain to plan a step-wise process in advance. Any problematic situation that allows for a delay between a stimulus and a response can be processed in the prefrontal cortex, increasing the chances of coming up with an optimal solution. Let's take a look at some of the most important functions of the prefrontal cortex.

Developing impulse control. "Impulse control" is a dry phrase. It doesn't convey how hard it is to stop yourself from lashing out at someone who has just angered you. Quite frankly, it often would feel good if you were to blast that person with nasty words or worse. A well-functioning prefrontal cortex is capable of stopping you before you strike out. It reminds you about the negative long-term consequences. This can take the form of waiting to demonstrate anger in order to receive a bigger payoff later. More often, and more ideally, controlling the impulse to lash out allows the anger to diminish so you can maintain important relationships over time.

Planning for the future and anticipating the consequences of actions. One question I often ask clients who are in the midst of anger is "What are you planning to do with your anger?" I'm surprised at how often I get only a surprised look in response, as if getting angry were an end in itself. Frankly, it's not very useful to be angry just for the sake of being angry. It's a waste of energy. Fortunately, the prefrontal cortex allows you to convert the raw energy of anger into an action plan. If you make a good plan, you have a decent chance of being able to deal effectively with whatever has upset you. One key is being aware of how others will respond to your actions. You can often use mental rehearsal to help with this. As you consider a possible action, ponder how your partner, your boss, your children, your friends, law enforcement, and society in general will react to your fantasized behavior. If the response would be adverse, you can adjust your plan accordingly. This particular skill involves comprehending the mental and emotional states of others, a key feature of empathy and a critical skill in anger management. We'll look at empathy in detail in chapter 8.

Extinguishing negative patterns. Although many things, including habitual anger patterns, can be learned unconsciously, unlearning habits almost invariably requires a conscious process. As mentioned in chapter 5, on neuroplasticity, real brain change begins when you make—and keep—a deep commitment to new behavior.

Adapting to changing circumstances. Lack of flexibility is one of the hallmarks of people who suffer chronic anger problems. It's easier for them to repeat a pattern of aggression, even if that usually produces poor results, than to consider alternative actions. Habitually angry people often fail to ask questions like "How is this situation different from similar ones I've encountered in the past?" and "What could I do differently this time so I won't get the same bad results?" Here, too, the prefrontal cortex (along with the anterior cingulate and the hippocampus) is key. It facilitates adapting to changing conditions and altering behavior when necessary. A well-functioning prefrontal cortex helps angry people come up with new ways to handle old problems. Above all, it allows you to learn from your mistakes so you can try something new the next time an anger-provoking situation arises. In addition, the prefrontal cortex allows you to make and keep a commitment to new behaviors over an extended period of time. This ability to stick it out is essential for promoting brain plasticity.

Tuning in to others' thoughts and feelings. The prefrontal cortex also plays a critical role in empathy, the ability to put yourself in the mind of others. When you ask yourself what makes another person think the way he or she does, you begin using the prefrontal cortex to understand the differences between the two of you. Empathy is a skill you can cultivate, and chapter 8 will help you do just that. When you have more empathy, you'll feel less angry when others do things differently than you would.

A Less-Than-Perfect Prefrontal Cortex

As I've said before, nobody has a perfect brain, and it's probably true that nobody has a perfectly functioning prefrontal cortex. Furthermore, getting angry seldom helps the prefrontal cortex work more effectively. Therefore, potentially anger-generating situations limit your reasoning ability twice over, as a poorly functioning prefrontal cortex makes it harder to handle anger-provoking situations well, and once anger is activated, the emotional power of anger limits your ability to deal thoughtfully with the problem.

At the extreme, some people suffer from serious prefrontal cortex problems, usually caused by genetic misfortune, brain tumors, disease, acts of violence, or accidents. These individuals can barely function in society and often wind up in prisons or mental institutions. Others, such as those diagnosed with schizophrenia, have serious cognitive difficulties but can usually carry on well enough to live independently. But it's far more common for people to have a few, more minor prefrontal cortex problems, such as poor memory, exhibiting poor judgment, difficulty concentrating, or inability to sustain goal-directed activity. They lead seemingly normal lives but occasionally run into problems that they handle badly. This is true of many people with anger problems. They get along well enough until they run into an anger-provoking situation. Then the prefrontal cortex seems to be impaired just when its function is most needed. I would guess that most people who have self-identified anger issues fit this pattern.

The most serious problems with poor prefrontal cortex functioning involve lack of impulse control. Many studies have shown a relationship between an underactive prefrontal cortex and a diminished ability to keep from acting thoughtlessly (Niehoff 1998). Acting thoughtlessly could mean driving recklessly, spontaneous drug abuse, or quitting a job on a whim. Worse, poor impulse control predicts violence (Niehoff 1998). When the prefrontal cortex doesn't work well, people are more likely to end up in trouble because they can't resist angry urges to hurt others. They can't say something like "Whoa, even though I want to throttle that person, I'd better not. It's not worth the trouble I'd get into." Instead, their thoughts are more along the lines of "I'm not gonna take this crap anymore!" And then they attack.

Here is a brief list of problems people have when the prefrontal cortex isn't working well. Since many of these are simply the flip side of the positive functions I described just above, I won't go into details:

- Lack of impulse control

- Inability to concentrate

- A tendency to obsess about problems

- Difficulty concentrating

- Inability to maintain focus and commitment

- Inability to plan

- Being overly emotionally reactive (because the prefrontal cortex can't counter the amygdala)

- Being inflexible

- Inability to understand or comply with social norms and expectations

- Difficulty tuning in to others' thoughts and feelings

- Generally making poor choices, particularly when angry

- Having an underdeveloped moral system and poor empathy

How the Brain Makes Decisions

Before I discuss how and why people with angry brains make bad choices, I'll first describe how the brain generally goes about the decision-making process. The first thing to note is that the brain is an action-directing machine. Trees and corn plants don't need brains because they don't move. But a spinal cord and brain are highly advisable for living organisms with a capacity for motion. With movement comes choice (unless the movement is entirely passive, such as when plants produce seeds that are blown to new soil by the wind). Our human brains allow us to move in many directions both in space and in time as we consider what directions we might pursue in the future. And as discussed, emotions are critical in this decision-making process because they tell us which possible future directions feel right and which feel wrong. Remember, the Latin root of the word "emotion" means "to move."

The human frontal lobes include both our most sophisticated mental processing networks and the motor cortex, which is the center for action, so that thoughts, emotions, and actions can be more easily integrated. However, it's useless to have a brain that can direct one's actions unless that brain has access to sufficient information about the world around it. The brain needs to gather information about the world, preferably lots of accurate information. Naturally, the brain has evolved a way to do just that. As by now you probably anticipate, it's a complex process. The brain uses *association areas* to integrate basic sensory information gathered bit by bit through the eyes, ears, and other sensory organs into a cohesive picture of what's going on and then develop and implement a series of appropriate actions. These association areas are responsible for our most sophisticated brain functions, such as perception, conscious thought, and goal-directed action.

Let's break this process down a bit: In gathering basic sensory information, the brain's sensory centers are never presented with a whole picture. The information they receive is more like the thousands of pixels that make up a television screen. Just as each pixel is sensitive to a particular signal, each neuron in the brain is amazingly selective. The sense organs activate many neurons, and each is sensitive to a specific signal. For instance, one neuron may fire when a moving object is 60 degrees above horizontal. But it fires only in response to exactly that angle, not 59 or 61 degrees. A nearby neuron fires in response to 61 degrees, and another nearby neuron fires at 59 degrees. The *primary sensory areas* in the brain are bombarded by these tidbits of data. It would obviously be impossible to make decisions at this level. You would be overwhelmed and paralyzed by a flood of undigested material.

Enter the association areas. First to get involved are the *unimodal sensory association* areas. Their job is to integrate all of the bits and pieces of information from any one sense organ. For example, the visual association region would collect and unify data about the color, shape, and direction of a moving object. This information then goes to a *multimodal sensory association area* that puts together data from all the senses. From there, this integrated information goes to a *multimodal motor association* area. The job of this higher-order brain region is to develop an appropriate movement plan. This plan is sent down through the *premotor* and *primary motor areas* for implementation. When we put all of this together, the sequence looks like this:

1. Your primary sensory areas independently gather bits of information about something happening nearby.

2. The bits of information gathered by each sense organ are collected and integrated at a unimodal sensory association area: Your eyes tell you that something is coming closer, and your ears hear increasingly louder noises.

3. This integrated information goes to the multimodal association area, which puts the entire picture together: "Oh my, that's a truck heading right toward me!"

4. The multimodal motor association area quickly comes up with an action plan: "Jump out of the way."

5. The plan is implemented by the premotor and primary motor areas.

How the Brain Turns Information into Action

Sensory information is received by the primary sensory areas

Unimodal sensory association areas

Multimodal sensory association areas

Multimodal motor association areas

Premotor cortex

Primary motor cortex

Physical actions

You might be wondering where or how actual decisions, such as "go down the less traveled path," are made within the brain. That's a difficult question because in many ways the specific task of decision making is a function of the entire brain. You might envision specific decisions as developing in the space between the multimodal sensory association areas and the multimodal motor association areas. Information from all sensory organs is fully integrated within the multimodal sensory association areas. The next step is taking effective action. Practically speaking, a decision is an action plan developed and then implemented by the multimodal motor association area.

Throughout this process, the brain's sensory association areas filter sensory information. This is necessary to avoid being inundated with a flood of data. It's impossible to separate information gathering from information filtering. This selective processing of data is particularly significant in regard to anger, as people with anger problems tend to both consciously and unconsciously filter out positive information about others, thereby sustaining a negative attitude.

Angry Thinking Is Bad Thinking

Let's tackle the question I asked at the beginning of this chapter: why do people make such bad choices when they're angry? The short answer is that the brain simply doesn't function well when a person is angry. As to the details, there are several key reasons: emotional overactivation; bias and selective attention; and habitual anger and negative plasticity.

Emotional Overactivation

Decision making can't be separated from feelings. Emotions almost always play a role in choices, especially when the decision is an important one. In making good decisions, however, people are informed but not controlled by their emotions.

Emotional overactivation occurs when the frontal lobes are hampered by a strong surge of emotion. Yet because the frontal lobes are impaired, you might think you can think just fine when you can barely think at all! It's extremely difficult to make good decisions when your head is pounding and your pulse rate is off the charts. You might get lucky sometimes, but all too often choices made while you're flooded with emotions lead to regrettable words and deeds. In essence, strong anger tends to lead to emotional overactivation, which further increases anger. When you're under the sway of this unfortunate feedback loop, you can lose control quickly.

All of the techniques you learned about in chapter 6—increasing bodily awareness, taking a time-out, deep breathing, progressive muscle relaxation, neurofeedback, and mindfulness meditation—can help keep emotional overactivation in check.

Bias and Selective Attention

When I was a sociology student, I learned a classic model of how information is supposed to flow in organizations. Bits of information were expected to flow upward from the employees with the lowest status all the way up to the topmost executive. Then that executive would make an informed decision based upon his or her ability to put all those pieces of information together and see the big picture. This decision would flow downward from level to level until finally it reached the lower-status employees, who would then (ideally) take action to loyally follow the boss's command. For example, Joe notices that sales of widgets have plummeted. Sally observes that sales of gizmos are rising. They both inform their bosses, who tell their bosses, who tell the big boss. "Aha!" says the chief, "It's time to convert our widget factory into a gizmo factory." She tells her immediate subordinates to get going on that job, and a couple of weeks later, Joe is making gizmos rather than widgets.

Unfortunately, no real organization works exactly like this, including the brain. Joe, for instance, may have been making widgets for so long that he can churn them out in his sleep. But Joe hates producing gizmos. So he hides the information about declining widget sales. Meanwhile, Sally wants a promotion, so she pumps up the sales report on gizmos. So the news the big boss hears is that sales of widgets are fine, and sales of gizmos are absolutely out-of-sight. Even now the situation could be salvaged if the boss would take a good look at the company's balance sheet. But she's a total optimist who attends to only the positive information in the books. She looks and sees exactly what she hopes to see, regardless of what is really there. Everything is going wonderfully, she thinks, so she orders her underlings to build three new plants, one for widgets and two for gizmos.

Joe and Sally sent biased data to their supervisors, and the big boss fell prey to selective attention when she ignored negative financial figures. The brain is vulnerable to similar errors of bias and selective attention. In fact, the skewing of reality begins before sensory information even reaches the frontal cortex. As you've learned, all sensory information (except smell) goes through the thalamus, where it is filtered for relevance. Incoming data is further filtered in the unimodal and multimodal sensory association areas. Data is also screened by the anterior cingulate, which is involved in detecting anomalies and working memory, before being transmitted to other areas of the prefrontal cortex. Then, as planned action sequences travel from multimodal motor association areas through several relay stations en route to your muscles, they get filtered as well. The result of all this filtering is that we are consciously aware of only a small percentage of the available sensory information. Plus, our awareness is slanted toward seeing, hearing, feeling, smelling, and tasting what we expect, rather than what is present.

Although it's limiting, all of this filtering is necessary. We would go insane if the brain didn't filter out most of the incoming sensory data. We couldn't take any action at all if we had to consider every potential option. We simply couldn't function without selective attention. It permits us to focus on what is novel and perhaps dangerous and ignore well-known or irrelevant information. But we do pay a price for selective attention when we fail to notice information that might allow us to choose a different path.

Even memories are subject to bias, selective attention, and other distortions. Recent evidence suggests that every time you revive a long-term memory, it will be slightly transformed (Kandel, Kupfermann, and Iverson 2000). Think of stories of the fish that got away, and how that fish became bigger and bigger in memory. Perhaps more to the point, think of how the more you think about an insult or slight, the worse that insult feels. You may also become more certain that the insult was intended and dislike the offender more as a result.

I see this frequently in therapy when people return to a specific memory over several sessions. I've noticed that these memories tend to become more emotionally biased: an initially negative memory becomes darker and darker over time, while a positive memory tends to become happier.

Also note that selective attention isn't limited to unconscious processes. It is both necessary and inevitable at the level of consciousness.

The bittersweet quality of selective attention is that while it allows us to focus upon a few things at a time, it also dooms us to being unable to attend to everything else that's going on.

Chronically angry people have a very specific selective attention problem that keeps them angry. Psychologists use the term *hostile attributional shift* to describe how chronically angry people distort the messages they receive from others. Here's how this pattern develops: When someone says something nice to them, they hear it as neutral. If someone says something neutral, they hear it as negative. And if someone says something that's actually negative, they hear it as a total attack.

For instance, Jill bakes a chocolate cake. Her boyfriend, Carlos, comes home and says, "Oh, a chocolate cake. That's yummy." Jill, who has an anger problem, doesn't take that as a compliment. She might hear it as a neutral statement ("He's talking about the cake, not me, the person who baked it"), or she might go directly to feeling insulted ("Well, yeah, obviously you care more about that cake than you do about me"). Now let's say Carlos makes a neutral statement, like "Oh, a chocolate cake." Jill hears that as a negative statement ("He must not like it"). And if Carlos is a little critical ("Oh, a chocolate cake. Why didn't you frost it?"), she'll hear that as awful ("He's saying I'm a terrible baker"). Next, Jill decides that Carlos isn't on her side—that he is, in fact, an insensitive lout who doesn't deserve any kindness or consideration from her. Decisions lead to action. There goes the cake onto the floor.

Chronically angry people don't think like this just on occasion; rather, the hostile attributional shift becomes a regular pattern. The effects of this way of thinking include having a dark view of the world, becoming more suspicious over time, expecting the worst from others, and acting in ways that confuse and punish even those who appreciate them.

You might be wondering whether this shift is conscious or unconscious. I believe the shift usually occurs below conscious awareness because it has become an automatic reaction, a habit of distorted perception. People are usually surprised when I first point this pattern out to them and give them several examples of how they engage in it. But even after people become conscious of what they're doing, the hostile attributional shift has immense influence. It takes dedicated, deliberate, ongoing effort to begin seeing good as good, neutral as neutral, bad as bad, and awful as awful.

Obviously, it's impossible to make good decisions when you regularly distort and misinterpret other people's intentions. Angry people with a hostile attributional shift are going to make many poor choices. They're going to respond as if they're being attacked when no attack is occurring or intended.

Habitual Anger and Negative Plasticity

Selective attention is actually a small part of a larger pattern I call *habitual anger*, a type of anger my wife Pat and I described in great detail in our book *Letting Go of Anger* (Potter-Efron and Potter-Efron 2006). The best way to describe people with habitual anger is that they are negative, grumpy, critical, and irritable. People with habitual anger have a negative, pessimistic outlook. They expect the worst from others and even from themselves. And, like Eeyore the donkey in *Winnie-the-Pooh* or the characters in the movie *Grumpy Old Men*, habitually angry individuals let everybody know about their negativity. They tend to be sarcastic and cynical, especially when others are trying to be nice to them. They are also quite critical because they're quick to find fault in others. They are characteristically irritable, always finding reasons to be at least a little upset over just about anything. At the extreme, habitual anger evolves into habitual hostility, a pattern in which people become mean-spirited and possibly violent.

Habitual anger is an excellent example of neuroplasticity in action; unfortunately, here the result is problematic, as people become trapped in a gray and ugly mind-set. Here are some typical characteristics of habitual anger:

- It is a product of thousands of repetitions.

- It becomes so automatic that people are unaware of their negative bias. They offer habitually angry responses without self-censorship or considering alternatives.

- It feels perfectly normal to respond negatively, grumpily, and sarcastically. There's a sense of "Yep, that's me" that goes unquestioned.

- It isn't responsive to the actual current environment. Often the habitual anger developed years before, perhaps early in childhood.

By the time I see angry people as clients, this pattern usually serves no good purpose. In fact, it gets in the way of developing positive relationships and friendships, getting promoted, and a host of other facets of life.

- It's hard to change this pattern of thinking and acting and all too easy to fall back into it, even when people want to alter the pattern.

The habitually angry person is set up to make poor decisions. For instance, he or she finds all kinds of reasons to decline positive invitations from others. Go to the party? *No way, I don't want to hang out with those jerks.* Make love? *I'd rather watch TV; at least the people on TV are attractive.* Habitually angry people tend to make poor decisions because they attend to only the negative aspects of opportunities.

Sometimes habitual anger becomes part of a relationship. Couples who come to counseling have often developed mutual patterns of habitual anger. As a result, they frequently indulge in what I call "here we go again" arguments. Whatever the topic—money, sex, child care, in-laws, alcohol consumption, and so on—it gets brought up repeatedly but is never resolved. In many ways these arguments are like well-rehearsed theatrical performances. The couple may have acted out their drama hundreds of times. Each partner knows all of the lines by heart. Still, they feel strongly about the situation and hurt each other with accusations and attacks. They don't realize that they're training each other to keep saying and doing cruel things. They probably never realize either person could bring a quick end to the drama at any time by changing their lines. Both partners need to find new, less habitual ways to negotiate their differences. They need to retrain their brains to look for the good instead of the bad in each other.

There's also a meaner side to habitual anger. Some of the people I treat for domestic violence display this pattern. Their habitual hostility makes them conclude that almost everyone is an enemy, including people who love them. Perceiving their partner as an enemy promotes acts of violence. When they strike out, they erroneously believe that they're defending themselves against their partner's aggression. The reality is that the filter of habitual hostility leads them to misinterpret what their partner said or did.

136

Thinking Better

To review, angry people make bad decisions because they are handicapped in three key ways: by emotional overactivation, by selective attention, and by habitual anger. Being aware of these factors is an important step in overcoming them. But you'll also need some tools for thinking more clearly and making better choices. There are two main directions to take: You can think more clearly if you recognize and neutralize your anger. You can also improve your ability to consider your options even when you're upset. The techniques below will help you do both.

Buying Time

In chapter 6, I recommended taking a time-out as a good strategy for those times when you realize you're getting flooded with anger. It's a good way to buy time. Other strategies include breathing mindfully for a couple of minutes or mentally counting to ten (or twenty…or even one hundred if need be). It's always important to slow down your thoughts, feelings, and actions when you feel angry, but you probably don't need to quit feeling angry altogether. After all, anger is like a messenger from the unconscious telling you to attend to something important. However, you probably do need to let that first surge of adrenaline go through you before you can communicate, negotiate, fight fair, or solve conflicts.

When I was in training, one of my mentors gave me an excellent piece of advice: "Ron," he said, "you tend to blurt things out too quickly. That's because you're sure that what you're thinking is important. Try waiting one minute before you say what you're thinking. Then, if it still seems necessary to say it, go ahead." I quickly learned that most of my "immensely significant" ideas that just had to be spoken immediately shriveled in importance in that single minute.

I understand that it can be very hard to keep your mouth shut for even a few seconds when you're angry and upset. But it's a good idea to do exactly that. I'm not encouraging you to shut down and say nothing at all when you're angry. The goal is to use your anger well and make statements that are informed by your emotions, not controlled by them. The bottom line here is that you should never make important decisions when you're significantly angry.

Choosing Whether to Accept Anger Invitations

An anger invitation is anything that happens, inside you or outside of you, that you *could* (but don't have to) get angry about. Your boss yells at you. A driver cuts you off. Your partner forgets your birthday. The porridge is too hot. The porridge is too cold. The porridge isn't right (no raisins!). The average person probably gets about a dozen anger invitations a day.

Angry people, especially those who are habitually angry, tend to selectively pay attention to anger invitations. It might be a bit of an exaggeration, but you could say that angry people never receive an anger invitation they don't want to accept. Furthermore, because their anger has become automatic, they often start reacting to these invitations before they consciously realize what's happening.

Noticing these anger invitations is crucial if you're habitually angry. You need to bring them into conscious awareness. Most critically, you need to realize that there is nothing written in stone that says you must accept an anger invitation. You really do have a choice. When you take the time to think about it, you'll almost assuredly choose to decline some anger invitations that you would have automatically and semiconsciously accepted before.

Here's a suggestion: Keep a notebook with you and record all of the anger invitations you receive in a day and what you choose to do with them. Over the course of a week, you'll probably discern some patterns. Perhaps certain types of anger invitations are easy to decline and others are more difficult. Also note the skills you used to successfully decline anger invitations. Those are probably worth cultivating and using more frequently.

The goal isn't to decline every single anger invitation you receive. It's to be consciously selective so you don't waste the power of anger on trivial or useless matters.

Seeking a Balanced Perspective

As mentioned previously, a classic approach in cognitive therapy is asking people to rate their thoughts on a scale of 0 to 10. In the case of angry people, the question might be "On a scale from 0 to 10, where 0 indicates not at all important and 10 indicates life threatening, how serious is this issue?" The scale usually looks something like this:

10:      **Life threatening.** Someone's health or safety is seriously at risk. Take immediate action.

8 to 9: **Very serious.** Something pretty bad could happen unless the issue is dealt with soon. But you can take time to think before you act.

5 to 7: **Troublesome.** The issue is disturbing. Perhaps it violates your values. However, it's not immediately dangerous. Slow down, think, and plan.

2 to 4: **Annoying.** You feel displeased and irritated. But the situation isn't really all that important. Maybe say one thing and then let it go.

0 to 1: **Trivial.** You're getting upset over nothing. Keep quiet and let it go.

Angry people tend to rate problems too highly on this scale. For instance, I once counseled a dad whose teenage daughter came home one day with her hair dyed green and black in honor of her high school football team's colors. He wasn't just a little upset over that. He was irate. He rated her behavior a 9 because she hadn't asked his permission first. He was stunned when nobody else in the group rated it higher than a 4 or 5. He then realized that he consistently became extremely angry with his daughter over small things. After that he was usually able to shift gears with the phrase "It's no big deal." He learned to develop a balanced perspective. As a result, he no longer reacted to trivial or annoying things his daughter did as if they were terrible attacks against him.

If you tend to overrate how dangerous or serious situations are, you'll become angry too often and too intensely. The solution is a five-step process:

1. Take time to think before you say anything.

2. Rate the seriousness of the problem or offense on the scale of 0 to 10.

3. Reconsider the situation to make sure your rating isn't too high.

4. If possible, ask others how they would rate the situation.

5. Respond with actions appropriate to the actual intensity of the problem.

Disputation

Disputation is a technique in which you challenge a negative way of thinking and replace it with a more positive thought. Here's an outline of how it works:

1. You receive an anger invitation—usually something someone says or does that you could decide you don't like.

2. You automatically accept the invitation and have negative thoughts about the other person's actions. These thoughts increase anger rather than calming you.

3. That leads you to say or do something that reflects your anger and may cause unnecessary problems.

4. You catch yourself starting to go in that direction, then stop yourself and come up with a way to think about the situation that reduces your anger level. This is the actual disputation.

5. That helps you calm down and make better choices.

Here's an example of how disputation might play out in real life, using a typical traffic incident:

1. A guy is driving only fifty-five miles per hour in the fast lane of the freeway. This is your anger invitation.

2. You think, "He's slowing me down. He can't do that to me!" This is a thought that increases your anger.

3. You honk your horn, he slows down more, you give him the finger, and so on.

4. You catch your negative thinking and replace it with a thought like "I'm not in a hurry, so why get upset?"

5. You calm down and wait patiently for a good opportunity to pass. You've made a better choice about how to respond to the situation.

Disputation may look easy, but it's actually pretty tricky. You can't forget about your emotions. Your disputation must possess emotional power for it to work. Otherwise you won't be able to substitute it for your original, anger-inducing thought no matter how much sense it makes. So in the example above, if you were really in a hurry, that particular disputation ("I'm not in a hurry...") won't work. And even if you have all the time in the world, that disputation won't work if your response is along the lines of "Oh, yeah, I suppose I should think that way." But perhaps a different statement would be more compelling, such as "This is no big deal," "Life is too short to get pissed off over little things," or "Cool it. I need to get home safely for the kids."

Disputations harness the power of selective attention. You train yourself to replace habitual thoughts that typically increase your anger with different interpretations of the same situation that reduce your anger. Notice that this doesn't involve selectively noticing one set of facts and ignoring others, like the big boss at that company making widgets and gizmos. Instead, you're consciously deciding which of many possible interpretations of a situation you want to accept. By consciously choosing to opt for interpretations that reduce anger, you can retrain your brain.

Disputation is a skill that improves with practice. You might need some help coming up with emotionally effective disputations at first, but you'll get better over time. It's a good idea to ask trusted loved ones and friends for their ideas. However, bear in mind that the disputation has to feel right to you, not just make sense. As you begin to use disputation regularly, you'll feel rewarded, because this technique works well. As a result, you'll feel more in control of your life every time you use disputation to calm yourself down and every time that leads to making better choices.

Summary

In chapter 6 you learned some skills and techniques for improving your ability to handle the first two stages of an anger episode: activation and modulation. These approaches helped bring some of the unconscious processes of an anger episode to consciousness. That laid the foundation for this chapter, in which you learned techniques to ensure you make better conscious choices: buying time, choosing whether to accept anger invitations, seeking a balanced perspective, and disputation. These approaches allow you to do a better job of handling the third and fourth stages of an anger episode: preparation and action. If you can avoid making bad choices during an anger episode, you're essentially home free—at least in the eyes of others. To all outward appearances, it may seem that you no longer have an anger problem. Still, it's important to learn how to handle the last two stages well—feedback and deactivation—so that you can learn from your anger episodes, respond more appropriately at every stage of anger episodes in the future, and fully release yourself from the vise grip of anger. One key skill can help you do all of that: empathy—the topic of the next chapter.

Chapter 8

Developing Empathy

The final two phases of a typical anger episode are feedback, which helps you determine whether your response to the anger episode was appropriate, and deactivation, or letting go of your anger so you can get on with life. In discussing these topics, I'll focus on two major ideas: empathy and forgiveness. Without empathy, the ability to understand other people's feelings, feedback from others would consist of only their words and outward actions. This kind of limited feedback is often superficial and even misleading. And without forgiveness, people might find it impossible to move on in their lives after suffering a painful emotional blow. Empathy also plays an important role in forgiveness.

Many people with significant anger problems have trouble with empathy and forgiveness. However, most people can improve their empathy skills with motivation and effort. Forgiveness is always possible (although it should never be considered mandatory), if and when people decide to move in that direction.

Empathy

Over the course of our species' evolution, the humans brain has become exquisitely sensitive to social cues. This allows us to observe other people's facial expressions and gestures and immediately sense, usually correctly, not only what they are doing, but also many of their thoughts, feelings, and intentions. That allows us to figure out what action we might take to help us get what we want while remaining in the good graces of our community. Some writers use the term "social intelligence" to describe this quality.

One skill lies at the very center of social intelligence: empathy. It is partly automatic and unconscious, but also partly a conscious choice. People who are born with good abilities in this area tend to get along well with others. People who are raised by loving, emotionally responsive parents usually become good at it. Sadly, some people don't have either kind of luck. Fortunately, though, the parts of the brain that help develop empathy are plastic. That means people can improve in this area if they're willing to make the effort. To help you gain a better understanding of empathy and how you might cultivate it, let's take a look at some key aspects of empathy.

Unconscious attunement in the brain. The ability to empathize begins at the unconscious level. As mentioned (and as I'll describe in detail later in this chapter), mirror neurons in the brain fire both when an individual makes an intentional movement (such as reaching for a pencil) and also when he or she observes another person making a similar movement. Although this kind of attunement is not empathy, it does provide a neurological basis for empathy.

Conscious effort by one person to understand another's inner world of thoughts, feelings, and intentions. This conscious skill can be developed and improved over time. At the neurological level, the frontal lobes become deeply involved whenever you try to understand another person's feelings, values, thoughts, and intentions.

Hypothesis formation. Part of empathy is making a series of educated guesses about another person's mental and emotional state. For example, you meet your best friend for lunch and she immediately begins to cry.

Before you say a word, your mind is mulling the possibilities: Is she crying from happiness that you're together? Has something awful happened that makes her sad? You're guessing about both her feelings (happy, sad) and their cause (spending time together, a bad event).

Awareness of similarities between oneself and the other person. Your own past experiences can be a major clue in developing an accurate awareness of what's going on with the other person. In the example of meeting your friend for lunch, you might remember times when you suddenly broke into tears: "When I cry like that, it's usually because someone died. Maybe she's crying for the same reason I cried. Perhaps someone close to her died." That thought brings back your own feelings of tearful sadness. You begin feeling emotions that might be similar to your friend's. In this case, you're using your own memories to guide how you respond to your friend.

Awareness of differences. Awareness of similarities isn't enough. "I know exactly how you feel because that happened to me" is a trap. Empathy involves remembering that each person's experiences are unique. Besides, you are still guessing about what's going on with your friend. Your hunch that she's crying because someone died may be entirely incorrect.

Nonjudgmental engagement with the other person. Empathy is an interactive process. A hypothesis is just a guess. To discover more of the truth, you sit down, reach over and take your friend's hand, and ask her what's going on. Then you give her your total attention, listening without interrupting. You allow yourself, including your thoughts and feelings, to be fully present with your friend. You suspend judgment because judging others disconnects you from their inner world. Gradually, your friend tells you that her boyfriend just broke up with her and she feels both sad and angry. So your original guess was partly correct. She is feeling sad, and she is dealing with a loss. But now you understand that she is also feeling angry and that the loss is due to a breakup, not a death.

A sense of deep connection. A successful empathic experience frequently culminates with both parties feeling closely connected with each other. They emerge with a clear sense that a bridge has formed between them. This bridge is partly emotional and partly in the realm of thoughts. However, it is only temporary. Empathy is always a work in progress, never a finished product. As you get to know someone, you'll be able to develop increasingly accurate guesses about that person's inner world, but they will always remain educated guesses rather than absolute facts.

Based on all of that, I'll offer a detailed, nuanced definition of "empathy": Empathy is an active, thoughtful process in which one person fully engages another with the goal of better understanding that person's inner world of thoughts, feelings, and intentions. The process involves developing informed hypotheses about the other's inner world and then improving those educated guesses by compassionately and nonjudgmentally seeking more information.

Even though that definition is quite detailed, a few clarifications are in order. First, note that mimicry (unconscious imitation of another's facial expressions and gestures) does not constitute empathy. And although sympathy (concern for another's pain) is related, it isn't empathy because it doesn't include putting yourself in the other person's shoes.

Also, many people think "empathy" refers solely to the ability to tune in to other people's emotions. However, you can't really separate people's emotions from their thoughts and actions. Remember, the word "emotion" literally refers to "motion," and motion implies action. To be truly empathic, you can't just attend to people's feelings. You must try to understand their way of thinking—their worldview. Part of that worldview includes their immediate intentions. And as it turns out (and as I've mentioned), the human brain has developed specific neurons that help us perceive others' intentions: mirror neurons.

There's one more term I need to define: *empathic concern*. This refers to the caring feelings we have when we tune in to others' painful emotions, coupled with a desire to help relieve their suffering. It's important to understand that empathy doesn't automatically lead to empathic concern. Still, the two obviously relate to each other. And as you might suspect, people with well-developed empathy also tend to readily display empathic concern.

For effective anger management, you need to develop both skills: empathy and empathetic concern. Each lessens anger in its own way. Empathy reduces anger because it diminishes negative judgments. Empathic concern reduces anger by substituting caring responses for aggressive reactions. Empathetic concern also ensures that empathy isn't used for negative purposes. For instance, unethical politicians, salespeople, psychologists, religious leaders, and people from many other professions could utilize empathy to manipulate and take advantage of people. After getting their victims to open up to them at deep emotional levels, they could pretend to show caring by responding to them emotionally. This sends the message that they understand their victims, which builds unwarranted trust, opening the door to manipulation, seduction, and betrayal. Empathy without empathic concern is dangerous, but empathy with empathic concern is healing.

Angry people tend to be relatively bad at empathy for many reasons, and I'll discuss those reasons a bit later in this chapter. For now, a key point is this: If you're having trouble with anger, improving your empathic ability could be the single best way to change how you relate to others. I'll describe several approaches to improving empathy skills at the end of this chapter. But first, let's take a look at the neurological underpinnings of this miraculous skill.

Two Components of Empathy

There are two distinct components of empathy, and a complete empathy experience integrates both of them. The first component, *affective attunement*, is also sometimes called *affective empathy* or *empathic attunement*. This aspect of empathy happens automatically. It primarily occurs as one person attends to another's facial expressions and bodily gestures. Most of this attention is at an unconscious level. When affective attunement is really working, the result is that the observer feels almost literally in touch with the other person's feelings and thoughts. Furthermore, both parties may sense a strong connection between them, a linkage of minds and emotions. Mirror neurons make this kind of empathy possible. Other parts of the brain associated with affective attunement include the insula, the anterior cingulate, the thalamus, the right inferior parietal lobe, and frontal lobe premotor areas. The insula, an older part of the cortex located between the frontal and temporal lobes, is particularly important because it acts as a relay system that connects mirror neurons with the limbic system.

The second component of empathy is often called *mentalizing*. You mentalize whenever you make an effort to figure out what someone else is thinking. In order to do so, you must temporarily let go of your own thoughts, feelings, and assumptions about the world. Instead, you imagine that you are someone else and attempt to place yourself into the other person's mental world.

Whereas affective attunement is primarily unconscious, mentalizing is just the opposite. It is a deliberate effort to understand the thoughts, feelings, and worldview of another person. The goal here is to take the perspective of the other person. For instance, a member of the Democratic Party might use mentalizing to reach a better understanding of just why his Republican friend values law and order so highly. Meanwhile, the Republican could be trying to comprehend why his Democratic buddy places such a strong emphasis on protection of the weakest members of society. However, neither will succeed in his quest if he becomes judgmental. Empathy requires that you maintain an open, noncritical mental stance.

Mentalizing uses somewhat different parts of the brain than affective attunement. There is more action in the medial prefrontal cortex, the right inferior parietal cortex, and both hemispheres' temporal poles. However, I don't want to give the impression that these two aspects of empathy are totally distinct. In reality, there is a great deal of interplay between them. The bottom line is that a person's overall empathic ability is a combination of these two processes. The better these two processes are integrated, the more empathic that person will be.

You may be wondering why the brain would devote so many resources to empathy—why so many regions of the brain are involved, and why both unconscious and conscious effort come into play. The single best answer is social survival. Human beings are social creatures. We need others to survive and to thrive. So it's in our best interest to know as much as we can about others' feelings, thoughts, and intentions. Empathy allows us to make educated guesses—hypotheses—about these things based on guidance from internal attunement mechanisms. The more skilled we are at empathy, the better our predictions become. In addition, we can use nonjudgmental engagement with the other person, along with other social skills, to move beyond hypotheses to understanding.

As mentioned, empathy is a skill you can develop and improve. In essence, you can train your brain to become more socially competent. While the firing of mirror neurons and other neurological mechanisms that allow empathy can't be controlled directly, you can learn to pay more attention and better attention to others. Making the conscious choice to do so will help increase your empathy skills over time.

The Origins of Empathy

As mentioned, empathy is a social survival skill. In a social world, it's extremely useful to be able to recognize others' feelings and anticipate their actions. Indeed, infants are born with the capacity for behaviors that allow them to eventually develop true empathy. The target of these early behaviors is their primary nurturer, frequently their mother. (In the discussion that follows, I'll use the phrase "mother-infant bonding," but I do recognize that many men are full or even sole participants in child-rearing.)

The mother-infant bond is amazing to observe. During feeding periods and at many other times, mother and child tend to unconsciously and automatically match each other's movements, emotional states, and facial expressions. As mentioned in chapter 1, the right hemisphere is first to develop after birth. Therefore much mother-infant bonding takes place within the right hemisphere, which tends to be more global and nonverbal than the left hemisphere. One important result is that, even once we reach adulthood, we may have difficulty putting into words our gut feelings about love, connection, and trust. Instead, we have a more of a global sense of those things.

Here's what early attunement looks like: The infant moves an arm and so does the parent. The infant murmurs and so does the parent. The parent smiles and so does the child. In fact, their movements, murmurs, and smiles are so well coordinated it often appears as though they are acting simultaneously. These coordinated states may be unconscious, but they are also usually quite satisfying to both participants. They produce a deeply felt sense of connection, an almost musical rhythm, a resonance that temporarily lifts the barrier between self and other. The positive result of frequent periods of such synchronicity is that the infant starts life with a strong sense that the world is a safe and caring place. The self-esteem of children so blessed is usually good as well, since they have a built-in confidence that others love them, take them seriously, and can be counted upon to understand. They are also likely to be interested in others when they grow up. This tends to come naturally when you feel at a gut level that people are on your side.

However, early attunement is not a form of empathy. One reason is that empathy demands clear boundaries. We must know the difference between ourselves and others in order to be empathic. Without clear boundaries, a person can become too involved with others' feelings and thoughts. This creates a merger of self and other, sometimes called emotional contagion. The person who says "I know exactly what you feel because I feel just the same" may be more involved in merger than empathy.

Of course, no parent can hope to be 100 percent responsive to a child. We all have good, "here I am" days and bad, "don't bother me" days. What's important for the development of empathy is that parents be responsive to the infant's signals regularly enough for the child to feel psychologically safe. Occasional, momentary lapses generally aren't damaging. In fact, they might be positive if the parent realizes there has been a breach of synchronicity and quickly repairs the damage. This sends the message that misunderstandings can be corrected and relationships can be mended.

Unfortunately, some parents consistently fail to synchronize their movements and feelings with the infant. They may be unable to connect at this core level because of abuse or neglect as a child, or perhaps because of more immediate issues, such as alcoholism, addiction, physical illness, or depression or other mental health conditions. In these situations, infants often have to rely upon their own resources. Because they have no one with whom they can connect, their empathic ability is not cultivated.

Mirror Neurons

What makes mother-infant bonding and the resulting synchronicity possible? The answer begins with mirror neurons. These remarkable structures allow us to respond to others' actions at the level of a single cell. Here's what happens: Someone you're watching makes a movement—not any random movement, but one that signals intention. For instance, the intention might be to pick up a glass of water. Instantly, some of the cells in your frontal and parietal lobes that fire when you make that same motion fire. Because your brain distinguishes you from others, not all the cells you'd use for that action fire, but enough do that it's almost as if you'd picked up the glass of water yourself.

Remarkably, mirror neurons act both as information receivers and action generators. More to the point in terms of this discussion, these neurons initiate processes that allow you to get a feel for another person's actions and intentions. This creates a bridge between you and the people around you. Basically, the existence of mirror neurons allows you to enter others' world with a fairly high degree of accuracy. In a limited sense, you come to know what another person is doing, feeling, and intending because you know what you do, feel, and intend in the same circumstance. However, this entire process is unconscious, automatic, and instantaneous. So it isn't the same as empathy because it doesn't include conscious effort to understand the other person. However, mirror neurons do lay the foundation for conscious empathy. They are necessary but not sufficient in themselves for the empathic experience.

As you learned in chapter 2, emotions elicit reactions (the "motion" in "emotion"). These action tendencies, such as the urge to run away when afraid or to remove an obstacle when angry, are intentions as well. As a result, emotional expressions are also tracked by mirror neurons. There is a specific brain pathway that connects mirror neurons with the brain's emotional center. Messages from the mirror neurons are routed through the insula to the limbic system, and especially to the amygdala. This pathway allows the brain to interpret the emotional significance of others' actions and expressions. Therefore, damage to the insula can disrupt this connection and limit a person's capacity for empathy.

The insula is a good example of how one part of the brain becomes involved in many apparently diverse functions. It has been linked with awareness of body states (such as heartbeat), experiencing negative emotions (including anger), meditation, eye-hand coordination, a sense of disgust, feelings of pain (both one's own pain and that of another), and even drug cravings.

Anger Disrupts Empathy

Let me begin this section with a thought experiment. Visualize yourself becoming extremely angry with someone. Then, simultaneously let yourself feel warmth and caring toward that individual. Additionally, put yourself into that person's shoes so you can take his or her perspective. If you're like most people, you'll find this extraordinarily difficult to do. That's because strong anger is virtually incompatible with empathy. Most people have to cool down a lot before they can experience affective attunement (feeling what others feel), mentalizing (cognitive empathy, which involves taking others' perspective), or empathic concern (caring about others once you feel their pain).

Many studies have demonstrated a negative correlation between empathy and anger or aggression. What this means is that the more empathy you have in any situation, the less likely you are to become angry and aggressive. In essence, empathy tends to inhibit anger and aggression. In the same vein, people who have higher scores on measures of trait empathy (meaning they display high levels of empathy across many different situations) are more likely to have lower scores on measures of anger and aggression (Vitaglione and Barnett 2003). Studies also indicate that anger is negatively related to other positive social characteristics, such as cooperative behavior, self-regulation, moral development, and generosity.

These correlations are interesting, but they're only patterns. So let's take a look at some of the concrete ways that anger disrupts empathy.

First, any strong emotion tends to inhibit good frontal lobe function. This makes it difficult to think calmly, and calmness is a necessary condition for empathy, especially for mentalizing (the cognitive aspect of empathy). The flip side of this dynamic is that by concentrating upon another person's feelings, thoughts, and intentions, you can probably energize the reasoning cortex while damping down more emotional regions, which will decrease angry reactions.

Second, it is particularly difficult to attend to other people's social signals, especially subtle cues, when you're angry. Angry people's bodies and minds are generally too agitated to handle emotional information flowing their way. Plus, the target of anger becomes more of an obstacle to be overcome than someone to understand. However, successful empathy demands being interested in and curious about others.

Third, as discussed in the previous chapter, angry people often display a negative thinking pattern known as the hostile attributional shift, misinterpreting others' messages and viewing them as worse than intended. It's hard to feel empathy for others when you mistakenly believe they're attacking you.

Fourth, people have a tendency to want to punish those they're angry with. So when they notice that the object of their pain feels physical or emotional pain, angry people are all too likely to continue or even redouble their hostility rather than stopping to comfort the other party. This is a barrier to empathic concern. I believe this happens frequently when someone on the receiving end of anger begins to cry or look sad. Sadness is a plea for understanding and comfort and normally brings people toward you. But many of my most angry clients tell me that they just get angrier when their target starts crying. They often mistakenly believe the person is trying to manipulate them. The statement "If you keep crying, I'll really give you something to cry about" clearly reflects this pattern.

Fifth, and finally, people sometimes resort to anger as a way to avoid feeling distressed because of another person's pain. When faced with another person's physical or emotional pain, people tend to consistently respond with one of two reactions: either they feel empathic concern and move toward that person in an effort to help relieve the pain, or they feel so much personal distress that they move away to relieve their own pain. So how can someone who is overly sensitive to another's pain keep from feeling distressed? Getting angry, which drives people away, comes in handy here. I believe that many people use anger this way—to keep people away so they don't have to feel their own emotional distress about other people's pain. Unfortunately, this defense limits their chances to get better at handling their emotions and improving their empathy skills.

Angry People Receive Little Empathy

For angry people, lack of empathy is a two-way street. In addition to regularly displaying poor empathy skills, they also often find that they don't receive much empathy from others. The most obvious reason for this is that the targets of their anger tend to withdraw from them. Who wants to take the time and effort to understand why someone is acting like a jerk? This creates a downward spiral over time. The angry person drives others away, then feels misunderstood and disliked as a result and therefore becomes even angrier, driving others even farther away. Anger, especially chronic anger, leads to physical and emotional isolation.

However, it isn't inevitable that a person's anger causes others to withdraw. It is possible to be empathic in the face of another person's anger. In fact, it's likely that the mirror neurons of the target of anger will be activated. Unfortunately, what that means is that anger sometimes begets anger. Anger seems to be a highly contagious emotion at the preconscious level. For instance, sometimes couples get locked into mutual anger and neither person can back away long enough to calm down. They become habitually hostile and habituated to conflict. As a result, each is so mad at the other that escalation toward violence becomes more likely.

Some people can handle another person's anger well, experiencing an empathic response but not an angry one. Instead, partly at an unconscious level, they sense the angry person's underlying pain, shame, guilt, sadness, loneliness, or fear and respond internally to those emotions. They may also try to put themselves into the angry person's shoes so they can better understand his or her perspective. As a result, they are able to respond to the angry person effectively and without becoming angry themselves. Professional therapists are trained to respond in this manner (although almost all counselors I know, including myself, occasionally find their own anger buttons pushed by certain clients in certain situations). But angry people are asking a lot when they expect an empathic response to their anger. You really can't expect a positive reaction to behavior that says, "If you really loved me, you'd ignore my anger, mean words, and cruel actions and treat me considerately."

Forgiveness

Resentment, empathy, and forgiveness are deeply interwoven. Resentments arise when people are unable to let go of perceived insults, betrayals, abandonments, and other psychological injuries. Resentment tends to develop in intimate relationships because it usually involves a betrayal of trust. Examples include repeated infidelity, betraying the trust of a friend by destroying his or her reputation with lies and half-truths, or cheating siblings out of their share of the family estate by getting a judge to throw out their parents' final will.

Most people would have trouble dealing with these situations. They might (appropriately) become angry, anxious, sad, or scared. They would probably find themselves repeatedly thinking about what happened. They might lose sleep over it or even get sick. They would almost assuredly feel resentful for a while. But many would suffer their pain and then find ways to let go of it. Eventually their anger would diminish. That's forgiveness at work. Forgiveness lets people back into your heart even after they've seriously injured you.

However, some people find it very difficult to let go of their resentments. In fact, their anger might even build over time. These people seem to become obsessed. They cannot stop thinking about and blaming the offender. They feel they can't get on with their lives until justice has prevailed. That might mean having an affair as payback, destroying a now ex-friend's reputation in retaliation, or destroying family property so the greedy sibling can't have it.

At this point, it should come as no surprise that certain brain regions are associated with forgiveness. Specifically, the anterior cingulate, posterior cingulate, left superior frontal gyrus, and frontal temporal region are all activated when we try to forgive. As discussed earlier in this chapter, the anterior cingulate is also a major component of the affective attunement circuit. This overlap implies that feeling the pain of the offender may be at the core of forgiveness. Forgiveness occurs when people who have been injured can remember the offender's good qualities, reexperience some of their positive feelings for the offender, and let the person back into their heart.

Perhaps this dynamic is best summed up in what one of my clients said about her ex: "Yes, he betrayed me. He cheated on me and that hurt. It still hurts. But now I remember the many good years we had together. I could keep hating him, but then I'd be renouncing all of those good years. Now I can think about him without crying in rage. I feel so much better now than when I was obsessed with how mean he'd been to me." In the end, forgiveness allows the injured person to heal.

Improving Empathy and Empathic Concern

Given that anger and empathy are inherently incompatible, if you have an anger problem and want to do something to change that pattern, you can accomplish a great deal by improving your empathy skills. The rest of this chapter is devoted to suggestions on how to do that.

Committing to Improving Empathy

As discussed in chapter 5, neuroplasticity, or the brain's ability to change, allows us to develop, maintain, and improve skills, including empathy, but only with sustained commitment. Indeed, improving your empathy skills is quite similar to improving your physical stamina through exercise or your physical health by altering your diet. In any of these situations you would need to make the goal a top priority in order to see improvement. And you'd need to keep that goal as a high priority over many months so your skills could evolve. The bottom line is that it takes steady effort to get better at empathy. You'll need to practice, practice, practice. But the payoff is huge. Eventually the neural networks that facilitate empathy will become stronger, faster, and more efficient. Empathic responses will become easier and more automatic over time as you develop the habit of empathy.

If you aren't sure if you're ready to make that strong of a commitment, consider three of the rewards of becoming more consistently empathic. First, you'll probably be less angry. When you tune in to others' thoughts and feelings, you'll better understand why they say what they do and behave as they do. Those reasons make sense from their perspective. Second, people respond favorably to empathic listeners. Empathy attracts, just as anger repels. If you would rather have people come toward you instead of walking away, becoming more empathic can help. Third, empathy is the bridge that links human beings. You'll almost certainly feel better connected with the people you love as you improve your ability to enter into their worlds.

In the remainder of this chapter, you'll find specific techniques for improving your empathy skills. Read through them, then put commitment to work by choosing one or two and trying them out for a week. If you find that your life and relationships get even just a little better, seriously consider making a six-month commitment to developing more empathy.

Paying Close Attention to Facial Expressions

One aspect of empathy, affective attunement, is primarily automatic and unconscious. Naturally, that makes it hard to directly improve affective attunement. After all, you can't give your mirror neurons an order to start working more efficiently. However, there is something you can do to help them work better. You can consciously remember to keep your eyes on other people's faces.

Remember that mirror neurons fire when one person observes another's facial expressions and physical gestures, particularly movements that signal intent. A fearful face predicts flight, so mirror neurons related to fear and flight fire when that face is observed. An angry face predicts aggression, and once again mirror neurons fire. (The target of that anger may, however, respond with fear, shame, or other such emotions; just because mirror neurons related to anger and aggression are firing doesn't mean the observer will take similar action.) These facial signals are rather obvious and fairly easily observed. However, many facial expressions are subtle. They may contain only hints of emotion or blends of emotions. It's very important to catch subtle but important signals, such as a brief sigh, a quick eye roll, a single tear, or an angry glance. Don't miss noticing these brief signals because you're caught up in your own thoughts—or because you're studiously observing your feet or the television or computer.

One caution: Watch carefully, but don't interpret excessively. Don't assume you know the meaning of every expression on other people's faces. Nonverbal information is easy to misinterpret, especially if you're angry. A brief sigh, for instance, may signal weariness, but it doesn't mean the person is tired of you or of dealing with you. Maybe that person is just plain tired. Likewise, a single tear could be a tear of joy, not sadness. Even when your mirror neurons are firing correctly, your conscious mind may override them with inaccurate interpretations.

It's also important to notice other people's gestures. Hand and arm movements are particularly expressive. You must watch for them as well if you want to improve your affective attunement.

Occasionally Copying Others' Expressions or Gestures

Imagine this scenario: You're talking with a friend and notice that she's furrowing her brow. You're puzzled by that expression. One way to explore its meaning is to furrow your own brow. As you do so, perhaps you'll realize that she's feeling confused. That could help you recognize that you forgot to give your friend some important background information. This is an example of how it can be helpful to consciously imitate other people's gestures (or tone of voice).

Be careful, though. If you overdo mimicking, others may think that you're mocking them. I recommend that you use this technique only when you believe it will genuinely help you better understand others.

Encouraging Your Curiosity about Others

Now let's move on to the second component of empathy, mentalizing, which is more intentional and thoughtful than affective attunement. You can build skills in this cognitive aspect of empathy more directly. The goal is to put yourself into other people's shoes and appreciate the way they look at life. You can make better sense of what others say and do by entering their world (though it's important not to lose track of your own).

There are specific techniques that will help you develop this skill. But first you must be motivated to do so. To assess your motivation, read the following statements and consider how much you agree or disagree with each statement:

- I think people are endlessly fascinating. There's no such thing as a boring person.

- Everybody has a story to tell that's worth my time and energy.

- My life will be enriched by taking interest in others, especially those who are closest to me.

If you are to improve your empathy, your answers need to be true, true, and true. Let's take these statements one at a time:

- **People are endlessly fascinating:** This is true if you make it true in your mind. If you expect people to be interesting, they will be. If you expect them to bore you to tears, they will do exactly that. It's a self-fulfilling prophecy. You can choose to expect boredom, but you'll never get better at empathy that way.

- **Everybody has a story to tell:** People's life stories are composed of both memories and myth. They focus on turning points in life:

births and deaths, successes and failures, marriages and divorces, choices made and paths not taken. Some people are eager to share their life story; others hold back. Eventually, though, almost everyone will share their story if you show genuine, nonjudgmental interest.

- **My life will be enriched by taking interest in others:** Human beings are social by nature. We wouldn't possess mirror neurons if our brains weren't programmed for connection. But anger often leads to disconnection, separation, loneliness, and isolation. If you put your anger aside long enough to take a real interest in others, you will almost certainly begin to feel more involved. You'll also probably feel good, at the deepest levels of your being, about that development.

Developing Good Listening Skills

Empathy is about listening as well as watching. Although listening may seem passive, it's an art—and a skill you can develop. Here are several tips on how to improve your listening skills.

Keep an open mind. Everybody has some biases. We don't live in neutral gear. We all have belief systems that we defend. However, empathy requires that you consciously put aside stereotypes, biases, and judgments. For example, maybe you believe that marriage is sacred, that higher education is useless, and that you should always try to be optimistic. Then you find yourself in a conversation with someone who doesn't believe in marriage, who values higher education, and who is a card-carrying pessimist. Here's what you need to do: Consciously put your beliefs in a little mental storeroom for a while. Remember that empathy demands you be interested in the other person's world, and enter into that world as best you can by asking questions and listening carefully. Throughout, avoid the temptation to argue or try to change the other person's mind.

Ask open-ended questions. Open-ended questions can't be answered with a simple yes or no. For example, "Will you be home by six o'clock?" is a closed question, whereas "When will you be coming home?" is open-ended. The value of open-ended questions is that they leave more room for people to tell their story.

Ask about other people's feelings, goals, values, life history, and self-perception. Don't stick to safe topics like "How are the kids?" or "Do you think it's going to rain?" Practicing empathy involves offering others an opportunity to reveal important aspects of their personality.

Be prepared to share your world. Just as anger begets anger, so does empathy beget empathy. When you try to fully understand others, don't be surprised when they return the favor. These people are likely to ask you questions and listen intently to your answers. Here, too, you have a choice. You can answer with vague generalizations or evade the question. However, I recommend that you do your best to respond, especially if you're trying to become less angry. Feeling truly understood and cared about is a wonderful antidote to anger.

Practicing Forgiveness through Empathy

Developing empathy for people who have deeply offended you is a good way to begin or continue forgiveness work. Here are some questions you can use to increase empathy toward those who have injured you:

- At the time of the offense, what was going on in the other person's life that might explain his or her actions?

- What positive things can you remember about the offender to help balance all the negative thoughts you have about him or her?

- How has the offender suffered in his or her life?

- How have you harmed others, both unintentionally and on purpose? Are you really all that different from the offender?

- Is it possible that you could forgive the offender as others have forgiven you for your offenses?

Using Anticipatory Empathy to Lessen Anger Outbursts

Earlier in this chapter I defined the term "empathic concern" as the caring feelings we have when we tune in to others' painful emotions, coupled with a desire to help relieve their suffering.

It is certainly possible to be empathic without extending empathic concern. This can be benign or neutral, as when people use empathy skills only to better understand others. However, as mentioned at the beginning of the chapter, in the absence of empathic concern it's possible to use empathy to manipulate others. Many a jilted lover has discovered too late that the person they believed to be a kind and loving partner was actually a sociopathic con artist.

While it is possible to be empathic without caring, I don't recommend it, especially if you're trying to become less angry. You need to let yourself care deeply about other people's pain. This will help you hurt them less often with angry outbursts. I call this kind of awareness *anticipatory empathy*, or *preventive empathy*. By caring about how someone would feel if you yelled at them or called them names, you can increase your commitment to staying calm. And if you do slip up and act angrily, your willingness to feel some of the other person's pain will help you make amends and renew your commitment to calming your angry brain.

Summary

Empathy is a powerful tool for managing anger. Although I opened this chapter by discussing how it can help with the final two phases of an emotional episode—feedback and deactivation—it actually helps at every stage. It's hard to get angry in the first place (activation) when you feel empathy toward the other person. If you do manage to get angry, empathy can keep your emotions at a more manageable level (modulation). And, of course, when you're motivated by empathic concern for the other person, it's unlikely that you'll plan or carry out aggressive actions against them (preparation and action). As you increase your empathy skills and apply them to all stages of your anger episodes, you're likely to find that feedback and deactivation aren't as much of an issue, as you increasingly handle anger episodes well and don't have excessive levels of anger to deactivate.

A Final Comment

Before you put down this book, I suggest that you read through chapter 5, on neuroplasticity, one more time. That could help you remember that transforming your angry brain into one that is calmer is both possible and difficult. You will need to make a deep and lasting commitment to change your thoughts and actions. But the take-home message is that you *can* do it. You don't have to live with an angry brain. You can change your brain and, in the process, improve your relationships and your quality of life.

Further Study

After digesting this volume, you might be tempted to learn more about the angry brain. In this section I'll briefly discuss some resources I recommend. Some of these are designed for the general public, while others are more oriented toward mental health professionals and may be more challenging to comprehend. I'll try to make this distinction clear for each reference.

If you're interested in learning more about the brain, I recommend two excellent sets of CDs put out by the Teaching Company: *Biology and Human Behavior* (second edition), by Robert Sapolsky, and *Understanding the Brain*, by Jeanette Norden. Robert Sapolsky's course also includes several lectures on human and animal aggression.

I used the highly respected book *The Principles of Neural Science* (fourth edition), by Eric Kandel, James Schwatz, and Thomas Jessel, to guide my writing about the brain's architecture and mechanics. Another formidably difficult but rewarding volume on brain science is *The Neurobiology of Aggression and Rage*, by Allan Siegel, one of the world's foremost experts on anger and aggression.

If you're particularly interested in the subject of mirror neurons, I recommend Marco Iacoboni's *Mirroring People*, a book written for the general public. For an excellent summary of research on empathy, check out *The Social Neuroscience of Empathy*, edited by Jean Decety and William Eckes.

Louis Cozolino, PhD, has written two excellent volumes on the brain: *The Neuroscience of Human Relationships* and *The Neuroscience of Psychotherapy*. These books are intended primarily for psychologists and therapists, but others will certainly find them illuminating.

If you're particularly interested in the relationship between anger and mindfulness, I recommend *Anger: Wisdom for Cooling the Flames*, by the Buddhist monk Thich Nhat Hanh. Or, for a more scientific approach, check out the work of Daniel Siegel. *The Mindful Brain* is especially illuminating, as it also gives a glimpse of a brilliant mind taking on the challenge of describing what happens to your brain when you meditate.

If you find the concept of neuroplasticity fascinating, you'll want to read *The Brain That Changes Itself*, by Norman Doidge. This interesting book, written for the general public, describes neuroplasticity in detail.

For a thorough discussion of how humans become violent and stay violent, and how to end the cycle, I recommend *The Biology of Violence*, by Debra Niehoff, which is written for a general audience.

The approaches I've outlined in this book should go a long way toward calming your angry brain. However, we can all always use more strategies for dealing with problems—including anger. For more tips, techniques, and exercises, check out some of my other books: *Angry All the Time*, specifically aimed at habitually angry people; *Letting Go of Anger* (with Pat Potter-Efron), which looks at eleven different ways people handle anger invitations; *Rage*, written for those who have serious problems with losing control of their anger; *Stop the Anger Now*, a workbook with many helpful exercises; and *Thirty-Minute Therapy for Anger* (with Pat Potter-Efron), which provides streamlined instructions for a variety of effective anger-management techniques.

Appendix

Medications That May
Help with Anger

With all of this book's discussion of causes of anger (especially in chapter 4), and particularly causes such as brain malfunctions or imbalanced hormone or neurotransmitter levels, you may wonder whether medications might sometimes solve the problem. Before I discuss medications, I want to offer a few cautions. First, I'm not a medical doctor, so what I write here should be understood as a summary of what doctors, patients, and researchers have described, not as me giving medical advice. Second, I am not promoting taking medicines as the first line of treatment for anger and aggression. I believe medication is appropriate primarily when people are desperate for help and cannot control their dangerous aggressive urges. Third, medications can have negative side effects, and this must be monitored carefully.

Nevertheless, the appropriate use of medications can help some people gain better control of their anger and aggressive tendencies. It can promote personal and family safety, help preserve and improve relationships, and increase self-esteem. Furthermore, effective medications can help people gain the time they need to develop and improve their anger management skills. Ideally, people would use medications just long enough to help them build these skills.

Just as there is no single cause for anger and aggression and no single center for them in the brain, there is no single medication that is always useful. Rather, any among a number of medications may help, depending upon the area or areas of the brain contributing to the anger problem. Frequently, the only way to find out what works is through trial and error, which is also necessary to identify the medications that have the least troublesome side effects.

Antidepressants

Low serotonin is a major cause of irritability and impulse control problems, including angry impulses. Since low serotonin is linked with depression, anyone with depression could have an anger problem and anyone with an anger problem may be depressed. The selective serotonin reuptake inhibitors (SSRIs) are a class of antidepressants that help keep serotonin in the brain synapses by slowing its reabsorption by the neurons that sent it into the synapse.

I've seen many people whose anger problems were significantly reduced or entirely resolved when they took SSRI antidepressants. Naturally, these medications don't work for everyone, but when they do they can change a person's life for the better.

Certain antidepressants are also prescribed to help people with obsessional thinking problems. People whose emotional gearshifts don't work well may benefit from taking these medications, which may help them more easily let go of their problems and quit worrying so much about things they cannot control.

Psychostimulants

It's hard for people to think well when they get angry. But imagine how much harder it is for folks whose frontal lobes are damaged or ineffective. They simply cannot problem solve or come up with alternatives to aggression when they most need to do exactly that. Such people often tell me that they can think of only one thing to do when stressed: get mad to drive people away. Since they have to do something and that's the only thing they can think of, that's what they do. Their inability to consider nonaggressive choices gets them into trouble again and again.

Psychostimulant medications such as Ritalin (methylphenidate), Cylert (pemoline), and Adderall (a blend of several amphetamines) are designed to help people better use their frontal lobes, allowing them to concentrate, problem solve, and consider their choices. When use of these medications is warranted, they can help people develop alternative strategies to anger and aggression.

Mood Stabilizers

Medications such as lithium are widely prescribed for people whose moods swing wildly from elation to depression, including those diagnosed with bipolar disorder. The greatest danger of violence usually occurs during the manic phase of a bipolar swing. This is the phase in which people feel passionately about positive things (and therefore can fall head over heels in love within minutes) but also about negative things, like perceived insults.

The people who see me for anger-management counseling and also have bipolar disorder describe how when they get mad during manic episodes they simply fly out of control. It's as if they're stuck in overdrive. All too often, rage is the result. When they take appropriate mood-stabilizing medications, they still become angry at times, but they are much less likely to blow up.

Anticonvulsants

As mentioned, the most severe attacks of blind rage seem to have many of the characteristics of a brain seizure. Indeed, antiseizure medications such as Depakote (valproic acid) and Lamictal (lamotrigine) can be lifesaving for people who can't keep from having these rages.

One person I worked with who benefited from these medications was Harlan, a thirty-five-year-old man who lived in a group home. His goal was to live independently, but every time he tried to do so he was undone by his anger and aggression. He simply couldn't handle the inevitable frustrations of independent living and would feel his rage building up over time. Eventually he would have an intense fit of rage, get arrested, land in the mental health ward of a hospital, and finally get transferred back to a group home. However, once he began taking an anticonvulsant regularly, Harlan discovered that he could make it on his own. He described very clearly how these medications made a difference for him: they gave him more time to think before he acted, and even more critically, they allowed his anger to subside instead of continuing to build up over time.

Antianxiety Agents

The brain's fight-or-flight mechanisms link anxiety with anger. I regularly encounter the results of this fusion among people whose excessive anxiety makes them jumpy, irritable, and defensive. So it would seem to make sense to try antianxiety medications, usually benzodiazepines, such as Valium (diazepam) and Xanax (alprazolam), to lessen both anxiety and the subsequent angry reaction.

There are three dangers, though. First, some people who take antianxiety medications develop an unpredictable and paradoxical rage reaction. Instead of calming down, they become irate and violent. Anyone using antianxiety medications needs to be aware of this possible side effect and should consult with a doctor immediately if this paradoxical reaction occurs. The second danger is physical addiction. People can build up a tolerance to these medications and then have trouble getting off them.

The third danger is psychological dependency. Frankly, this happens because antianxiety medications work too well. That may sound a little odd, so let me explain: At first people take a pill only in the midst of an anxiety attack. Because that works so well, next time they may decide to take the pill a little earlier, at the beginning of an anxiety attack. Next they take the medication even sooner, to prevent any symptoms from developing. The end result is concluding that they need the antianxiety agent to survive anxiety or just to feel normal. These thoughts create a psychological dependency. What had been merely an aid to living is viewed as a necessity.

Antipsychotics

Few physicians would prescribe antipsychotics, such as Seroquel (quetiapine), Zyprexa (olanzapine), or Geodon (ziprasidone), for the average person with anger problems. These drugs are simply too strong and have too many side effects. However, these powerful medications can be helpful for people who suffer from schizophrenia or other serious illnesses that impair thinking ability. Over the years I've counseled several people who tried all other approaches, both medical and nonmedical, to control their anger and aggression, to no avail. Almost inevitably, these people agreed to take antipsychotics only as a last resort. These medications didn't always work wonders, and sometimes they didn't work at all. Still, several of my clients have told me that they knew they would be in prison or dead without them.

Sleep Medications

I've had many people report to me that the single best remedy for their anger problems is a good night's sleep. Since many angry people do suffer sleep deprivation, at least in part because their anger and anxiety keep waking them up, it is possible that short-term use of sleep-promoting medications could be beneficial, helping sleep-deprived people get back into healthy physical and mental routines (which should include exercise and a good diet). However, sleep medications can produce the same kinds of physical and emotional dependency problems as antianxiety medications, so I encourage clients to talk with their physician about whether to take them.

Summary

I want to repeat what I said at the beginning of this appendix: I am not a doctor. If you have an anger or aggression problem, please confer with a physician before agreeing to try medications and don't make the decision to do so lightly. Go over all of the possible side effects and make sure that the people you love and trust know what you're doing in case something goes wrong. Because these drugs affect how your mind works, you may not realize that there's a problem. And even if you try medication and it works well, make sure you diligently apply yourself to learning nonmedical ways to handle your anger. I believe people need all the anger management tools they can develop. That way, if one fails they can reach for another.

References

Brefczynski-Lewis, J., A. Lutz, H. S. Schaefer, D. B. Levinson, and R. J. Davidson. 2007. "Neural Correlates of Attentional Expertise in Long-Term Meditation Practitioners." *Proceedings of the National Academy of Sciences* 104(27):11483–11488.

Cozolino, L. J. 2002. *The Neuroscience of Psychotherapy: Building and Rebuilding the Human Brain.* New York: W. W. Norton.

Dobbs, D. 2009. "The Science of Success." *Atlantic Magazine*, December.

Doidge, N. 2007. *The Brain That Changes Itself: Stories of Personal Triumph from the Frontiers of Brain Science.* New York: Penguin Books.

Dutton, D. 1998. *The Abusive Personality: Violence and Control in Intimate Relationships.* New York: Guilford Press.

Ellis, L. 2005. "A Theory Explaining Biological Correlates of Criminality." *European Journal of Criminology* 2(3):287–315.

Kabat-Zinn, J. 1990. *Full Catastrophe Living: Using the Wisdom of Your Body and Mind to Face Stress, Pain, and Illness.* New York: Delta.

Kandel, E. R., I. Kupfermann, and S. Iverson. 2000. "Learning and Memory." In *Principles of Neuroscience*, edited by E. Kandel, J. Schwartz, and T. Jessell, 1227–1246. New York: McGraw-Hill.

Moyer, K. E. 1976. *The Psychobiology of Aggression*. New York: Harper and Row.

Niehoff, D. 1998. *The Biology of Violence*. New York: Free Press.

Potter-Efron, R. T., and P. S. Potter-Efron. 2006. *Letting Go of Anger: The Ten Most Common Anger Styles and What to Do about Them*, second edition. Oakland, CA: New Harbinger.

Sapolsky, R. 2005. *Biology and Human Behavior: The Neurobiological Origins of Individuality*. Chantilly, VA: The Teaching Company. Audiobook.

Siegel, A. 2005. *The Neurobiology of Aggression and Rage*. Boca Raton, FL: CRC Press.

Vitaglione, G. D., and Barnett, M. A. 2003. "Assessing a New Dimension of Empathy: Empathic Anger as a Predictor of Helping and Punishing Desires." *Motivation and Emotion* 27(4):301–325.

Ronald Potter-Efron, MSW, PhD, is director of the anger management clinic at First Things First Counseling in Eau Claire, WI. He is author of many books about anger, including *Angry All the Time, Letting Go of Anger, Rage,* and *The Handbook of Anger Management.*

St. Louis Community College
at Meramec
LIBRARY

MORE BOOKS *from*
NEW HARBINGER PUBLICATIONS

ANGRY ALL THE TIME, SECOND EDITION

An Emergency Guide to Anger Control

US $16.95 / ISBN: 978-1572243927

Also available as an e-book at newharbinger.com

LETTING GO OF ANGER, SECOND EDITION

The Eleven Most Common Anger Styles & What to Do About Them

US $16.95 / ISBN: 978-1572244481

Also available as an e-book at newharbinger.com

30-MINUTE THERAPY FOR ANGER

Everything You Need to Know in the Least Amount of Time

US $15.95 / ISBN: 978-1608820290

Also available as an e-book at newharbinger.com

THE HIGH-CONFLICT COUPLE

A Dialectical Behavior Therapy Guide to Finding Peace, Intimacy & Validation

US $16.95 / ISBN: 978-1572244504

Also available as an e-book at newharbinger.com

WHEN GOOD MEN BEHAVE BADLY

Change Your Behavior, Change Your Relationship

US $16.95 / ISBN: 978-1572243460

Also available as an e-book at newharbinger.com

CALMING THE EMOTIONAL STORM

Using Dialectical Behavior Therapy Skills to Manage Your Emotions & Balance Your Life

US $16.95 / ISBN: 978-1608820870

Also available as an e-book at newharbinger.com

newharbingerpublications, inc.
1-800-748-6273 / newharbinger.com

 Like us on Facebook

Follow us on Twitter
@newharbinger.com

(VISA, MC, AMEX / prices subject to change without notice)

Don't miss out on new books in the subjects that interest you.
Sign up for our **Book Alerts** at **newharbinger.com**

ARE YOU SEEKING A CBT THERAPIST?

The Association for Behavioral & Cognitive Therapies (ABCT) Find-a-Therapist service offers a list of therapists schooled in CBT techniques. Therapists listed are licensed professionals who are members of ABCT and who have chosen to appear in the directory.

Please visit www.abct.org and click on *Find a Therapist*.